Contents

Foreword

Early childhood settings are dynamic and creative places in which to work. They are places where staff have little time away from the children to talk or reflect on what they do. Over the last 10 to 15 years workers in these settings have had to respond to the demands of constantly changing legislation and new developments in social policy. They have had to learn how to articulate their beliefs about how young children learn best and what constitutes quality care for children under 8. Many books have been written to inform practitioners of these developments. It is, however, *adult performance* and *adult relationships* within early childhood settings which are critical to the delivery of high quality services to children and their parents. Very little has, as yet, been written about the specific challenges of organising and working in a team to provide high quality education and day care for children from 0–8.

The great strength of *Working Together for Young Children* is that it offers current and intending early childhood workers a better understanding of how to lead a team and of the day-to-day organisational tasks within each setting. In a clear and realistic way it examines the work that goes on there and considers the constraints and strengths within the many different kinds of settings. Staff groups can work with the case studies to enhance their understanding of appropriate procedures and realistic boundary setting. The book also provides a clear model of what research tells us is good practice in child care, such as the 'key worker' system. It makes many useful recommendations, such as how to respond judiciously to centrally constructed government guidelines. It reminds us that, as early childhood educators, it is important to provide a broad and balanced curriculum where children's self-esteem and self-efficacy are central. It also reminds staff that they have an obligation both to listen to parents and to help them find a voice and become advocates for their own children.

It is a value-driven book. At a time when it would be only too easy to lose sight of the important principles that underpin early childhood education and care in this country, it should help readers to stay in touch with what is really important. What we need are confident and competent practitioners with a good understanding of the needs of young children, led and managed by challenging and supportive senior staff who are able to work in partnership with parents to promote the highest quality education and care for all our children. I hope very much that this book will help you in your studies. As early childhood workers you are part of a proud profession and therefore need to be rigorous and reflective practitioners.

Margy Whalley
Director of Research, Development & Training
Pen Green Centre for Under-5s & Their Families

Acknowledgements

We are grateful for the discussions with our many contacts in early years services. We would especially like to thank Ann Robinson, Information Officer of the Early Childhood Unit at the National Children's Bureau for her help in searching the literature. It is also long overdue for Jennie to thank the staff of Balham Library for their efforts in tracking down many books over the years.

Thanks to Jen Dunford and Maxine Thornborough for their helpful feedback on the first draft of the book.

Lance took all the photographs in the book. Most were taken at the Balham Leisure Centre crèche and the Balham Family Centre. Thank you to all the staff, parents and children who were involved. Our daughter, Tanith, drew all the sketches; we really appreciate her time and effort.

About this book

The aims of the book

Good practice in the different early years settings can depend as much on the skills of working well with other adults as on direct work with babies and young children. The book covers the application of good communication skills in working with colleagues and parents, the importance of assertiveness in working relationships and the development of teamwork. You will also find guidance for facing difficult situations in meetings, confronting poor standards and dealing with conflict between individuals. High standards also require attention to how a centre is managed on a daily basis and to the policies and procedures which will ensure quality in the service.

This book will support you as you work for good practice. You will find a wealth of information, practical suggestions to apply and ideas to provoke your own thoughts. Examples take account of the different types of early years settings: local authority children's centres, family centres, private nurseries, community-run and workplace nurseries, playgroups, the nursery and reception stages within schools and after-school or holiday play provision.

Much of the book's content will also be relevant and helpful if you are working in a residential children's home. Some parts of the book will help if you are working on your own, as a nanny or childminder, although the context is mainly that of working alongside colleagues.

Who the book is for

The content and approach of this book assume that you already have some experience of working with children and their families. You are likely to be a senior worker and may be the manager of your early years centre. This book will be a useful resource to you in managing an early years centre or in being an effective member of an early years team.

The book will also support you as you work towards qualifications in early years work. The content and approach of the book will help your study for National and Scottish Vocational Qualifications (NVQs/SVQs) in child care and education, up to and including level 3. Details of links to NVQ/SVQ qualifications are given in Appendix 1. The book will also be useful if you are working towards the NNEB or BTEC diploma or the GNVQ in health and social care.

How to use the book

You can use this book on your own to extend your own knowledge and examine your practice. You could also use much of the material as a resource in guiding your own early years team.

If you are studying for one of the early years qualifications, your supervisor will guide you as you use the chapters of this book to support your learning in particular topics. Many of the activities, as well as the ideas within the book, will be that much more useful to you if you can discuss the issues with your supervisor, with colleagues and, where appropriate, with parents and other users of your service.

You will need to build up a portfolio of your work for many of the early years qualifications. Activities in the book will help you to develop evidence of what you have completed in your work and the key issues involved. A habit of keeping clear notes of events and experiences will help you to focus your learning and improve your practice.

Terms used

Different traditions have led to a varied terminology for settings within child care, education or playwork. We have used the following terms in the book:

- *Worker* is used to cover any person who is working in an early years setting.
- *Manager* is used for the person who is in charge of the centre on a daily basis.
- *Centre* is used for any of the different kinds of establishment that offer a service to young children and their families. The short examples and case studies in the book are drawn from this range.
- *Parent* is used to mean any adult who is taking parental responsibility for a child and forming a relationship with early years workers. The term covers children's birth parents, foster or adoptive parents and other relatives or carers who are taking parental responsibility.

Workers, parents or children can, of course, be female or male. In order to avoid repetition of phrases like 'he or she', we have most often used the plural. You will find that the examples include male and female and it will be obvious in any section of the book when the sex of individuals is an important part of the discussion.

The case studies

Six early years centres appear in case studies throughout the book. The places and people are fictitious. However, the incidents and dilemmas have all been developed from real experiences of early years workers, parents and children. To help you link the examples, each centre has a logo which appears by the case study:

- Farm Road Nursery Class

- Gables Community Nursery

- Mount Park Children's Centre

- St Mark's Playgroup

- Salmon Lane Private Nursery

- Walton Green Family Centre

1 Organising an early years centre

This chapter covers:

- policies and procedures;
- administration and record keeping;
- finance and budgets;
- admissions of children;
- planning work with children.

1.1 Policies and procedures

All early years centres need to be open and honest about how they approach the work with children and families. It is good practice to write down the key issues rather than to depend only on spoken communication.

- *Policies* lay out key principles that inform and guide work.
- *Procedures* give the details of the steps that must be followed.

Legal requirements, for instance in employment or health and safety, will influence some policies and procedures. Primary legislation is usually supported by guidance from the relevant government department. The guidance for the Children Act, for instance, is very detailed about standards and your own local authority should have published their own guidelines. Your centre's policies and procedures will be checked through inspection under the Children Act 1989 or through quality assurance systems.

Policies

Your centre should ideally have written policies on all of the following:

- The principles of equal opportunities in the work of the centre. Equality should be a feature of all the other types of policies listed here, yet it can be helpful to have a written document that pulls all the issues together.
- Admissions to the centre, including how any waiting list is operated.
- Positive handling of children's behaviour and your approach to discipline.
- Partnership with parents and what this means for this centre.
- Early years curriculum in work with the children.
- Health and safety for workers, children, parents and any visitors.
- Personnel policy for workers and volunteers.

Writing policies

Policy statements need to be brief, but will be more than just a few sentences. Policies should be written in clear language, avoiding specialist terms wherever possible.

Policies should not be drawn up and finalised by just one person. Ideally these are the result of consultation involving workers and parents, as well as line management. If your centre has a management committee, this body may draw up your policies. Other sources of help are:

- your local inspection team (under the Children Act 1989) may have guidelines on the policies they expect to find in any centre;
- other early years centres in your area may have policies that could support you as you draft one that is relevant to your own centre. However, private nurseries in competition with each other may be less willing to share in this way;
- national organisations publish material that can be very helpful as you identify the key issues and weigh up different wordings.

Reading on . . .

★   Brock, Susan L. and Cabell, Sally R. 1989: *How to Write a Staff Manual: A guide for managers* (Kogan Page).
★   The *Guidelines* booklets published by the Pre-school Learning Alliance.
★   The *Starting Points* series of the National Early Years Network.

Legal issues

Some policies and procedures have to be written to take account of legal requirements. If you are in any doubt, then you must check. Consult your line manager and relevant local and national organisations.

Reading on . . .

★   Commission for Racial Equality 1996: *From Cradle to School: A practical guide to racial equality in early childhood education and care* (available from Central Books, 99 Wallis Road, London E9 5LN, tel: 0181 986 4854).
★   London Voluntary Service Council 1994: *Voluntary but not Amateur: A guide to the law for voluntary organisations and community groups* (LVSC, 356 Holloway Road, London N7 6PA, tel: 0171 700 8107).

Different languages

Policy statements, like any written material about your centre, should be translated into the main languages spoken by local families. Depending on where your centre is, this may be a simple or a daunting task.

You may be fortunate in having bilingual workers in your team or some of the children's parents may be able to help. There may be translation services available locally, although this could involve a fee. It will be important to discuss the ideas with anyone who is helping you with the translation, since very literal translations can lose subtleties of meaning.

Policies into practice

Even the best drafted policy statement does not, of course, do the work for you. Effective work requires that the team has a shared understanding of what is meant by a policy and that all workers are committed to putting the details of the policy into practice. Policies should be reviewed through discussion within the team and in consultation with parents.

CASE STUDY

Farm Road Primary School, of which the nursery class is a part, has a commitment in the school brochure that '*We value all children regardless of their ethnic or cultural origin and aim to promote tolerance in the school*'. Several staff have objected, saying that the wording is half-hearted and that one sentence does not make an equal opportunities policy.

Efforts have been made to extend resources such as books, play materials and posters. However, a recent review of the school's policy on behaviour highlighted that teachers and helpers were uncertain how to challenge racist and sexist remarks between children. Then a parent governor raised the concerns of several families that the school assumed everyone was nominally Christian unless specifically told otherwise – to the point of writing this description in the children's records when parents had deliberately left the relevant box blank.

The next closure training day was devoted to setting a framework within which an equal opportunities policy could be developed over the following months. The day was attended by the entire school staff, all the governors and led by a local education advisor. Everyone worked hard to produce a draft value statement and key areas. Two staff or governors took responsibility for each area, with the agreement to report back to a staff meeting in one month's time. The following notes were written up and circulated.

Value stance: 'In Farm Road Primary School we respect all adults and children equally and treat them as individuals, taking positive account of ethnic and cultural origin, religious belief, gender and disability.'

Areas of application

How can we make sure that our policies, procedures and practice are:

1 Free of discrimination or inequalities, whether we intended this or not?
2 Actively promoting equality and understanding?

We need to explore these two points in all the following areas:

- Our admissions system and how we promote the school.
- How we attract and select teachers, nursery nurses, support and administrative staff.
- Our curriculum – including the nursery – and all the resources for children's learning.
- How can we develop a positive approach to bilingual children and parents? (Some of our books in the staff room talk of 'children with little language' when they mean children fluent in a language other than English.)
- The school's Positive Behaviour Policy and that this is not coping with offensive name calling. Are we also missing racist or sexist bullying?
- Assumptions about religious belief – our administrative systems, school assemblies and celebrations throughout the year.
- Do we have reliable information that reflects the diversity in pupils, their families and our own staff group? If not, how can we improve our systems?
- How we organise for children with disabilities – access, appropriate curriculum and partnership with their parents.
- Anxieties among staff about children with serious health problems, e.g. the panic over Stefan's epileptic fit. What would be a positive approach?
- Assumptions about food and a healthy diet. For instance – complaints from vegetarian children that some dinner staff call them 'fussy'. Reactions to Muslim pupils who fast during Ramadan – do we understand the importance of this to the children?

In exploring all of these areas we need to continue to consult all the staff, talk with the children and their parents and with professionals working with the school and in the neighbourhood.

Questions

1 If your centre is still working towards an equal opportunities policy, take some of the issues above and make notes relevant to your particular setting.
2 An equal opportunities policy is not a one-off activity but needs to be regularly reviewed and discussed. If your centre has a written policy, consider two ways in which the review process could be improved. For instance, how wide is your consultation? How do you listen to children's views?

Of course, any policy has to be put into practice in a realistic way

Reading on . . .

These publications support early years workers to consider putting principles into practice and to communicate with parents and other carers.

★ Derman-Sparks, Louise 1989: *Anti-bias Curriculum – Tools for empowering young children* (National Early Years Network).

★ Henderson, Ann 1995: *Behaviour in Pre-school Groups* (Pre-school Learning Alliance).

★ Melville, Sandra 1994: *Gender Matters: A guide to gender issues and children's play* (Playboard).

★ Slabey, Ronald G. and others 1995: *Early Violence Prevention: Tools for teachers of young children* (National Early Years Network).

Procedures

Clear procedures support responsibilities in work without removing the personal approach important for good practice with children and families. Two examples are given in this section: health and safety, and child protection. You will find admissions in section 1.4, disciplinary procedures in section 4.4 and complaints in section 5.3.

Health and safety

In any centre there are potential risks to the well-being of children and adults. You will need clear procedures for a range of health and safety issues. These procedures should be written and be easily accessible for workers or parents to consult. Some issues will be directly relevant to parents, for instance, that the centre is a non-smoking area. Other issues are central for workers, for instance, non-negotiable rules about safe storage of potentially dangerous materials (such as cleaning fluids) and a schedule for health and safety inspections of the centre.

Your building can be welcoming as well as secure

CASE STUDIES

 1 Mount Park Children's Centre

The centre has included a paragraph about discipline in the booklet that they give to parents when their children start at the centre. The paragraph reads:

'In Mount Park we treat all children with respect and no child is ever smacked or treated roughly. Staff respond positively to the children, using techniques of encouragement. We deal with difficult situations involving children by using early intervention and re-direction. We set boundaries for acceptable and unacceptable behaviour.'

A recent discussion in the parents' group showed that all the parents understood smacking was banned in the centre, but most of the parents were confused about exactly what was done as an alternative.

1   What are the main ideas that the Mount Park team are communicating about a positive response to children's behaviour?
2   How might the written statement be re-drafted in more everyday language?
3   It can be easier to see the flaws in the policies of other centres. Look closely at a policy statement from your own centre and check on how clearly the ideas are expressed. You could ask for parents' feedback and show the policy to friends who do not work in early years.

 2 Gables Community Nursery

Over the last year the Gables team have been looking closely at their approach to girls and boys through the daily play activities. The team decided to take a more active line in encouraging play across sex-role boundaries. Keith, the centre manager, adjusted the rota to ensure that male and female workers did not fall into stereotyped roles. The team rewrote the equal opportunities policy with more emphasis on anti-sexist practice. The new policy was displayed with photographs of recent projects with the children.

Over the next fortnight five parents asked to speak with Keith. Two fathers were concerned that letting their sons dress up would make the boys gay. The remaining three parents took the firm line that the nursery should respect their wishes that their children follow traditional sex-roles. All the parents pointed to the nursery's policy on partnership with parents and the commitment to respect families' religious and cultural traditions.

1   What are the main issues that Keith and his team face with this dilemma?
2   Encouraging children to step across firm sex-role boundaries can offend families from a range of cultural or religious backgrounds. How can this aspect of good practice be compatible with partnership with parents and respect for traditions that the team does not choose to follow?
3   Describe a similar dilemma faced in your own centre. How were the conflicting obligations resolved?

Part of the induction process for new workers and volunteers should be a discussion about how regular and less usual events are to be handled. For example, it is important that all workers follow the same rules of hygiene when clearing up urine or blood and laundering children's soiled clothes.

Some procedures can be reproduced briefly as a reminder notice. For example:

● a 'Now wash your hands' notice in each toilet;
● instructions prominently displayed on what to do if the fire alarm sounds; (There should, of course, be regular fire drills.)
● a schedule for maintaining kitchen hygiene.

Health of children and workers
An early years centre is bound to have outbreaks of illness among the staff and children. Health and safety procedures are a good example of how one part of good practice in early years work can be dependent on other aspects of the daily routine. For instance:

- workers can reduce the chance of spreading disease by cross-infection. Strict procedures on hygiene in the kitchen are as important as personal hygiene of workers and encouraging the children in a healthy routine;
- if children should become ill, or have an accident, you will need to contact parents. So, it is crucial that children's records are complete, with contact numbers for parent(s) and emergency back-up numbers;
- you need to let parents know that there have been, for instance, cases of measles or head lice in the centre. You can pass on this information by a well-placed notice or by giving photocopied letters to every family. You would *not* identify the actual children affected. Your local health authority would advise you on how long children should be kept at home for particular illnesses;
- some illnesses, such as scarlet fever, have to be notified to the local health authority. Close cooperation will also be very important if you suspect a dangerous illness such as meningitis, or if you are assessing who needs to know that an individual child has hepatitis or is HIV-positive.

Insurance

Early years centres have to carry different kinds of insurance:

- Employers' Liability insurance is compulsory for any business or service that has employees. The certificate has to be displayed in your centre.
- Public Liability insurance covers injury or accident to members of the public in your centre. Some centres choose also to hold Personal Accident insurance which provides limited compensation for injury where no negligence is involved.
- Contents insurance – for the moveable items in the building.
- Buildings insurance – for the structure.

✠ CASE STUDY

The team at St Mark's Playgroup have a health and safety policy and procedures for children's illness and accidents. They were confident they had covered all the key issues until an unpleasant incident brought home the fact that they had overlooked the safety of the playgroup workers themselves.

The playgroup operates in the church hall of St Mark's. The telephone is in an office at the back of the hall and there is no extension in the main body of the hall. Sally, the playgroup manager, was the only worker left in the hall on a dark winter afternoon when she was confronted by a stranger who became verbally abusive when asked to leave. The man ran out when Philip, a volunteer at the group, returned unexpectedly for his bag.

In conversation among the team the next day, it was agreed that the rota should be adjusted so there would never be less than two people in the hall. This was to be made effective immediately.

The incident was discussed in the next playgroup team meeting and it was agreed that Sally would raise the team's concerns at the next management committee meeting. Suggestions were made that there should be a telephone extension in the hall and/or a panic button system installed. Sally also made a note to find out when the church council would be fulfilling their promise to improve the poor lighting on the pathway to the hall.

1 Are there any other issues arising from this incident that the St Mark's team should consider?
2 In your opinion should they tell the parents about the incident and, if so, how would this best be done?
3 What procedures does your centre follow to ensure the safety of the workers?

You may not be responsible for choosing the insurance company or making payments. However, managers and staff should be aware of the existing insurance and any requirements that arise, for instance, on security of the building. You will find further details about insurance in some of the booklets suggested on page 12.

Child protection

Every centre needs a procedure for child protection. Perhaps your own team is convinced that 'that kind of thing doesn't happen round here'. Unfortunately, ill-treatment of children crosses all the social and cultural boundaries; it would be very irresponsible to ignore this issue.

You may find that your local social services or educational authority has practical guidelines that could become the basis of procedures in your centre. You will find guidance in the publications listed in 'Reading on' below.

The main points in child protection procedures include:

- Signs of possible physical, emotional or sexual abuse in young children. These should be described carefully, since any assessment of risk should be made on patterns, rarely on the basis of single indicators.
- The kind of response expected from workers who see signs of possible abuse in children for whom they are responsible. The main points are that workers should neither start investigations nor confront parents on their own. They should consult a senior worker.
- The appropriate behaviour for heads of centres when abuse is suspected, including seeking a reasonable explanation from parents.
- If no reasonable explanation is forthcoming or the pattern is disturbing, the procedures should include a contact name and number for the local child protection officer or the NSPCC.
- Factual written records should be kept.
- The details of a family situation should be confidential. If the centre has a management committee, the chair should be kept informed by the centre manager.
- Additional procedures may have to be followed if a child is already on the local child protection register.
- Procedures should recognise that workers involved with families suspected of abuse also need support – both for their feelings and with practical help if they have to appear in court. The needs of staff should not be overlooked in an understandable concern for children.
- It should also be clear in procedures what course of action is to be followed if a member of staff is accused of child abuse.

Reading on . . .

★ Lindon, Jennie and Lance 1993: *Caring for the Under-8s: Working to achieve good practice* (Macmillan).
★ Wilson, Avril 1993: *Child Abuse: A guide for early years workers* (National Early Years Network).

ACTIVITY

Check the procedures on child protection of your own centre.

1 Do they cover all the points above?
2 Are you clear about the appropriate course of action in different circumstances?

Talk with two or three of the less experienced members of your team and discuss the extent to which they understand what they should do.

If your centre does not have child protection procedures or they need reviewing, then contact your local authority or NSPCC for guidelines in helping you to draft procedures.

1.2 Administration and records

Good practice in keeping records

Any system is only as good as the people who operate it and their attention to detailed, timely recording. Neither a beautifully crafted file index system nor an impressive computer package will complete and update themselves.

Paperwork

The amount and type of administration will vary depending on the centre in which you are working. If you work in a nursery class, then the school secretary will handle much of the administration and financial systems. The manager of a private nursery or a playgroup leader may personally complete the majority of the paperwork relevant to daily running.

Paperwork can become a daunting pile unless dealt with promptly. It must be clear who is responsible and what should be done. There are four possible ways to deal properly with paperwork:

*   *Act on it* – some written communications will require that something is done, for instance a request for monthly attendance figures at your centre.
*   *Pass it on* – a centre manager may read a communication and then hand it to the person responsible for this issue. Perhaps a letter is relevant to a parent's complaint and so is passed to the parent liaison officer.
*   *File it* – reports or letters about children may need to be placed in the relevant folder. Material about centre policies needs to be filed logically.
*   *Throw it away* – some material may be irrelevant circulars or can be put in the bin when the relevant information has been taken out.

You need a system that eases filing and finding

TO THINK ABOUT

Any centre needs clear guidelines on the life of any written material. Your management committee or other body may decide for how long you should keep records of children in your centre. The Inland Revenue and other external bodies have rules about how long you should keep financial records.

1   Consider at least three types of record in your centre and find out for how long they should be kept.
2   When you dispose of any paperwork, what steps do you take to ensure that confidential material is properly destroyed?

Understanding the details

With any system of records you need to be clear about the following:

*   What kind of information is needed for the records?
*   How should it be recorded and in how much detail?
*   Why is the information being recorded? It is good practice to understand the reasons, particularly if you need to explain to a colleague or parent.
*   Who should have access to the information? Are there particular guidelines about how access is given?

ACTIVITY

Consider one kind of record that is regularly completed in your centre.

- Treat each of the points on pages 8–9 as questions posed about this record and note down the answers.
- Discuss with one or more of your colleagues whether any improvements could or should be made to the current system.
- Imagine that a serious flu virus kept the worker(s) who complete the records at home. What should be in a written set of instructions to enable a colleague to complete the work?

- To what extent does all or some of this information have to be passed on and to whom?
- Are there any time deadlines by which the information or a summary must be passed to the appropriate person or department?
- How are the records stored? What steps are taken to ensure that they are secure and only accessible as appropriate?

It will always be important to find the answer to your questions about records you are asked to complete. It is much safer to get a clear answer than to work on assumptions that may not be correct.

Systems of record keeping should be reviewed from time to time since improvements are possible. However, you should not change a system without checking on reasons for the current method and discussing proposed changes with others who use these records.

In any centre it is risky if only one person knows how to complete a given kind of record. Before there is a crisis, you should write out clear instructions and keep these with the record itself.

Records on computer

If any of your centre's records are on a computer, then it is crucial that anyone who might have to assume responsibility knows how to get into the relevant computer file, how to update it and, if necessary, print out. It is wise practice to make a back-up disk of any records and to update this every time the main file is changed. Otherwise, a computer malfunction can leave you with scrambled records, or none that can be accessed without a high level of expertise. It is good practice to protect sensitive information with passwords, known only to appropriate staff, and to agree who is responsible for updating records and when.

If your centre holds computer records of personal data (on workers, volunteers, children or parents), then it is a legal requirement that the centre is registered under the Data Protection Act 1984. Whatever the policy of your centre about access to records, this Act gives people the right of access to their personal data held on computer.

For further information

★ Contact the Office of the Data Protection Registrar, Wycliffe House, Water Lane, Wilmslow, Cheshire SK9 5AF, tel: 01625 545745.

Records on children and families
Individual records

Early years centres should open an individual record for children when they are about to start attending the centre. An example is given in the box.

 **EXAMPLE**

Salmon Lane Nursery – Children's record

Name: Daniel Ship

Admission date: 27.11.95

Date of birth: 10.1.90

Address: Flat 2B, Lakeview Mansions, Woodbridge

Parents: Mark Ship (father), Elizabeth Bailey (stepmother)

Contact numbers: Mr Ship 0386 772280 (mobile), Ms Bailey at 01246 9000, ext. 33. In emergency, Daniel's grandmother, Mrs Irene Shipovich, can be contacted on 01246 7734 and can pick Daniel up from nursery.

Family G.P.: Dr Verma, Woodbridge Health Clinic, Broad Lane. Tel: 01246 8945.

Medical details: Immunisation record is complete, including Hib. Pre-school booster immunisation due this year.

Childhood illnesses: Chicken pox in March 1993. Possibly German Measles (not confirmed) June 1995.

Family background: Mr Ship and Ms Bailey are Jewish (not orthodox). The family is English-speaking. Mrs Shipovich is bilingual in English and Polish. Issues relevant to Daniel's care discussed on entry – see diet and note 2.

Diet: Daniel should not eat any pork products or shellfish.

Special health needs: Daniel often gets tonsillitis. Please inform parents if he complains of sore throat.

Notes:

1   Mr Ship has legal custody of Daniel. Daniel's mother, Mrs Lyn Ship, is not allowed to pick Daniel up from nursery.
2   The nursery's approach to religious festivals was discussed with Mr Ship and Ms Bailey. Since the nursery celebrates five major religious festivals including Hanukkah, they were pleased for Daniel to take part in all the celebrations.
3   Parents have signed the consent forms for emergency medical treatment and the general outings form.

Reports on children

In some centres there will be much more information in the children's files than the basic personal background given in the Salmon Lane Nursery example. There may be summary reports of children's development, reports of medical and developmental checks and other material relevant to work with the child.

Reading on . . .

For more on reports about children and their progress you can consult:
★   Bartholomew, Lynne and Bruce, Tina 1993: *Getting to Know You: A guide to record keeping in early childhood education and care* (Hodder and Stoughton).
★   Griffin, Sue 1994: *Keeping and Writing Records: A step-by-step guide for early years workers* (National Early Years Network).
★   Lindon, Jennie and Lance 1993: *Caring for the Under-8s: Working to achieve good practice* (Macmillan).

Attendance register

An attendance register should be taken at the beginning of every day or session. This record is important in several ways:

●   An accurate attendance register is part of taking responsibility for a child and can be crucial in an emergency.

All groups, including short crèches, need records

- A register shows if a child attends only infrequently. You might contact the parents to check if they really want the place, especially if the centre has a long waiting list.
- You may have to inform Social Services if a child on the child protection register has not arrived at the centre. Part of the contract with the family may be that the child is brought to the centre every day.

Staff records

Any centre should keep a register of staff or volunteers for each day (or session) and a personal record covering:

- name and address of the worker;
- date of birth;
- contact and emergency telephone numbers;
- qualifications and experience;
- starting date at the centre and hours of work;
- relevant medical details.

Medical details might include a note of checks required to work at the centre or important advice concerning a medical condition of the worker.

All workers, except those who are involved on a voluntary basis, will have records of salary, income tax and national insurance. In a playgroup or private nursery, the centre manager may complete and hold these records on site. The records for a local authority centre or a nursery class may be completed and held elsewhere in the personnel department.

Accident book

An accident book should be completed for every accident. An entry should be made as soon as possible after the event and should include:

- date and time of the incident;
- name of the child(ren) or adult(s) who were injured or directly involved;

- circumstances of the accident, described factually with details;
- nature and extent of the injury as observed by workers. If necessary, a doctor would make a medical diagnosis later;
- what actions were taken and by whom;
- confirmation that parents or other relevant persons have been told.

Accidents that you successfully avoided would not usually be entered into the book. However, some incidents might raise safety issues that should be discussed in the team and perhaps with parents. For example, perhaps Jamal very nearly hit his head badly because the dressing-up box had been moved to beneath a low shelf; or two young children were caught just as they pulled open the nursery gate, which yet again had not been latched properly by the last parent to leave.

Reading on . . .

★ The Pre-School Learning Alliance publishes booklets on administration. You will find advice and possible layouts for records in, for example: *Pre-schools as employers*, *Accident and incident book* and *Accounts book*.

Access to information
Security and confidentiality

All families and staff should feel confident that personal information is not made public, either because records are left lying around or because their contents are discussed inappropriately. Centres need lockable filing cabinets or cupboards for storage. Files should be replaced as soon as a worker has finished completing an entry. You could use a tagging system to show who has the file if a worker removes it temporarily.

If your records are on a computer, the screen should be positioned so that people cannot glance at the information. Records should not be left on screen when the person working on the file leaves the room.

Difficulties for parents in access to information mean the process is not 'open'

Records such as the accident book or items like the petty cash box and voucher book should have a safe storage place. All workers should know the location and such items should not be left lying around.

Access and sharing information

Systems to keep records secure from prying eyes should not limit people's rights to look at the information in their own personal file. Parents should be able to consult and check the information about their child and their family. Staff should be able to look at their own records.

Some centres have specific procedures to follow when access is requested. It is usual practice to remove any third party information in a file, that is any letters or reports that have been written by bodies other than this centre. Third parties, such as health care professionals, can give permission for their material to remain in open file. Some local authorities and organisations follow a policy that material goes on open file unless the other person specifically refuses.

CASE STUDIES

 1 Farm Road Nursery Class

Moira is the assistant at Farm Road Nursery Class. As part of her NVQ studies she is exploring the way that Farm Road deals with parents' access to their children's records. Moira has interviewed all teachers and the parents with children in nursery and reception classes.

- The school head and almost half of the teachers preferred the system when children's records were not open to parents. The reason given was that they now felt wary about writing critical remarks.
- Most teachers believed that parents were not interested in seeing the records, since few had made a specific request.
- Nearly two-thirds of the parents interviewed were either unaware that they could ask to see their children's records or felt this was only something parents did when there was trouble with the school.
- Six parents in Moira's sample had asked to see the records. All were told by the head, 'There's nothing really interesting in the files. We tell you anything important'. Four parents felt unwilling to persevere. The other two completed a written request and then had to read their children's record with the head present in the room. Both parents told Moira that this made them feel that they were not trusted.

1   In theory, Farm Road has a policy of open access on children's records. What comments would you make on how this policy works in practice?
2   What realistic steps could Moira take to improve the current situation?

3   What is the procedure in your centre for access by parents to their children's records and any reports? Think of two ways, even minor, in which the procedure could be improved.

---

 2 Salmon Lane Private Nursery

Salmon Lane is a private nursery, one of three owned by Amanda, who is herself a qualified early years worker. In their weekly meeting, Debbie, the centre manager, asks to discuss appropriate sharing of information, following some recent incidents:

- One worker had given a child's immunisation record over the telephone but had not first checked the credentials of the caller. Debbie had taken over the call and established that the caller was the child's health visitor.
- Another worker had experienced difficulty in stopping a parent who was talking loudly in one of the group rooms about how 'Owen's mother has a terrible drink problem'.
- Debbie has given students on placement access to the children's records but is now wondering if she should have first asked the parents' permission.

1   What issues are raised by these incidents?
2   What steps should Amanda advise Debbie to take?
3   Consider any recent incident in your own centre that has highlighted better ways to handle personal information.

1.3 Finance and budgets

Financial records

Good records are vital to the financial accountability of a centre. Whatever your exact responsibilities, there are some practical guidelines for any kind of financial record:

- Lay out the account books with headings and space to make the entries clearly. Write legibly and make any corrections clear.
- Have a system for keeping all the receipts for expenditure, evidence of orders and copies of the receipts that you issue for income, for instance from fees. One approach is to fix together all the paperwork, organised into different types of income and expenditure, and to file it in a labelled envelope on a weekly or monthly basis. Piles of paper in a drawer are a recipe for financial disaster.
- Follow a system for promptly entering income or expenditure. The longer this task is left, the greater the risk that vital pieces of paper are lost or the source of a pile of cash has been forgotten.
- Income should be entered in a different section from expenditure and everything totalled up on a regular basis – weekly or monthly, depending on the records that you keep.
- You cannot reclaim the VAT on purchases unless your centre, or the funding organisation, is registered for VAT. Some people believe that registered charities are automatically exempt from paying VAT, but this is **not** the case. Businesses that are VAT-registered have to charge VAT on their services. Consult your local VAT office (Customs and Excise) or an accountant about VAT issues.
- Accounts should be checked by someone who is not directly involved in the centre. If you are in a private nursery, the company's accountant will go through the books at the end of the financial year. Playgroups, who do not have to be audited, may still choose to bring in an independent

Financial entries should be made promptly

person so that playgroup finances can be seen to be straight. If your centre is run by a local authority then the Finance Department will be responsible.

TO THINK ABOUT

Faced with financial records, people tend to veer between too much worry or an overly relaxed approach. It helps to think that you are marking up *a financial trail* that someone else can easily follow. The signs should be clear, for example, as to what each item means, where the petty cash receipts for March are filed or the nature of the bad debt that you are writing off.

In the box you will see simplified versions of part of one month in the records of a playgroup. Full accounts would have more entries and types of entry. The examples provide a sample layout and show how totals give a quick picture of the source of any income or how it has been spent.

Payment of staff

In local authority centres or nursery classes all responsibility for payment of staff may rest elsewhere. However, managers of private nurseries, of playgroups or small community nurseries may have to deal with income tax on the PAYE system and national insurance. There are strict rules and time deadlines that have to be followed. Look at *'Reading on'* on page 12 for publications that will help you.

 **EXAMPLE**

Cash book – St Mark's Playgroup 1996–97

Income: February 1996

| Date | Description | Total | Types of income | | |
			Fees	Fund-raising	Sundries
1	Balance brought forward	57.20			
2	Fees	12.00	12.00		
5	Fees	6.00	6.00		
5	Sponsored walk	15.00		15.00	
7	Donation from Slaters	30.00		30.00	
9	Refund from milk bill	7.80			7.80
	Totals	128.00	18.00	45.00	7.80

Note:

The fees from parents are also recorded in a separate book, giving the names of parents and tracking any payments that are still due. (Any centre which charges fees needs a clear policy on non-payment.)

Expenditure : February 1997

| Date | Description | Cheque no. | Total | Types of expenditure | | | |
				Rent	Food	Play materials	Repairs
5	Hall rent for 1–28 Feb.	052	40.00	40.00			
6	Sainsbury's	053	23.90		23.90		
7	NES order	054	30.00			30.00	
7	Blakemore's repair of cassette recorder	055	18.70				18.70
9	Unigate milk bill for 3–7 Feb.	056	25.00		25.00		
	Totals		137.60	40.00	48.90	30.00	18.70

Note:

The playgroup manager has requested monthly bank statements and checks these as soon as they arrive.

It is not a problem that the expenditure in February is higher than the income because the playgroup has reserves in the group's bank account.

Petty cash

| Date | Description | Total | Postage | Types of expenditure | | |
				Travel	Play materials	Sundries
1	Balance brought forward from Jan.	35.00				
5	Postage	2.50	2.50			
6	Plastic straws	0.90				0.90
6	Coloured paper	3.15			3.15	
9	Philip's travel expenses 3–7 Feb.	4.40		4.40		
	Total	10.95	2.50	4.40	3.15	0.90

Amount remaining in petty cash box: £24.05

Note:

The playgroup set up a system of petty cash when it became clear that paying for everything by cheque was leading to high bank charges. They agreed that petty cash was only to be used for items under £10.00 and that every item had to be recorded with a signed petty cash voucher, filed with the receipt.

The petty cash is reconciled at the end of every month, making sure that what should be in the cash box is the same as what actually is available in cash.

After three months of using a petty cash system the team reviewed the system. They agreed that they needed better forward planning on the group's use of stationery and sundries. Panic buying meant that the cost tended to be higher than thinking ahead and ordering from a bulk supplier.

Inventories and ordering

Early years centres need a workable system to keep track of stored materials of any kind. There are three main reasons for keeping an inventory:

1   You need to know when stocks of play materials such as glue or crayons are getting low. The same concern is necessary for consumables such as food and drink for the children, even if you only provide snacks. Attention to the inventory will enable you to re-order before the stores are empty.
2   You need also to keep a record of how swiftly a particular item is used. Perhaps there is a good reason for the high usage of coloured paper in your centre, but you might discover that workers unintentionally use the most expensive paper for almost every art activity.
3   An inventory should also be a record of the state of repair of larger items in the centre, such as play equipment, furniture or domestic machines. As far as possible, your inventory should act as a warning that a particular item will soon fail to meet appropriate safety standards for the children's play or that this repair to the sofa in the staff room is the last possible mend.

Setting and keeping to a budget

All centres have to keep expenditure within limits, ensuring that it does not exceed the centre's income or the budget set by the organisation in charge. Depending on your working situation you may be given an overall budget or a budget limit each year for different types of expenditure. You may be a member of the committee that plans and agrees next year's budget.

Preparing a budget

Effective forward planning of budgets uses past experience, along with predictions about the future in order to develop a realistic plan. A budget has to cover estimates for both income and expenditure.

Accurate records of previous years are essential to estimate the likely cost of providing snacks and drinks for the children, or the amount of art and craft materials that the centre uses over a twelve month period. You would check the records of expenditure and the inventories of materials (how much was used and how much is still left in the store).

Estimated income
There will always be some uncertainty in forecasting the centre's income for the next financial year, but the estimate must be as accurate as possible. Expected income will include fees paid by parents for their children's attendance and will assume that patterns of attendance are similar to past experience. Another source of guaranteed income might be from grants given by the local authority or charitable trusts. On the other hand, check to see if this previously secure source of income is under threat.

Estimated expenditure
It is usual to assess separately the *fixed costs* of running a centre from the *variable costs*.

Some sources of expenditure are fixed, regardless of how many children attend. Rent and local rates must be paid, as must the workers' salaries and the utilities (gas, electricity and telephone). Other costs such as food and drink, laundering costs and, to some extent, the buying of play materials will vary according to how close the centre is to full attendance.

Some estimate must also be made for the cost of buying any large items of equipment during the year. Again, an effective inventory system should warn you about likely costs. Perhaps the indoor climbing frame should be replaced within the year, or the washing machine may be making ominous noises.

Keeping in budget

The annual budget will have to assign the expected income to cover the various sources of expenditure. It will then be the responsibility of the centre manager to monitor expenditure month by month to ensure that the budget limits are kept.

Reading on . . .

This publication will help if you are responsible for raising funds:
★   Sewell, Liz 1994: *Cheque Lists: Statutory funding for early years groups* (National Early Years Network).

1.4 Admissions of children

Information about the centre

A leaflet or brochure should be made available to inquirers. This information should help parents to make an informed choice about whether to send their children to the centre. You might also receive enquiries from other early years professionals.

Written material on the centre's work is one way of communicating with parents in detail about what the centre offers and what is expected from parents in return. A brochure should never be expected to take over from face-to-face conversation; it acts as another channel of information.

An introductory leaflet should include:

- the main aspects of work at the centre, including opening hours and activities available for the children;
- key principles that guide that work;
- the admissions process;
- fees;
- name and telephone number of the person to contact for further enquiries.

The leaflet should be written in plain English and be available in all languages spoken by local families. There is little point in cramming an introductory leaflet with too much detail. Some centres find it better to have an additional information booklet for parents whose children have actually joined the centre.

An admissions policy

Any early years centre has to have an approach to admissions. The details of a policy will describe at the very least:

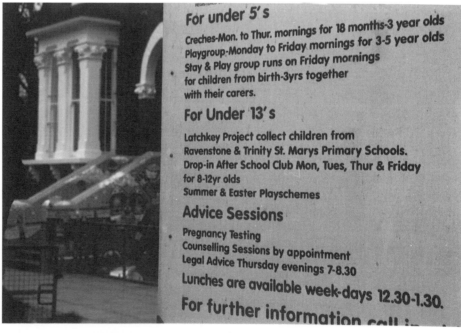

A board can provide basic information for all visitors

- the age range of babies and children who can be admitted to the centre.
- the total number of children who can attend at any one time.

If your centre is inspected under the Children Act 1989, then these two points will be a specific part of the registration of the centre.

Variety in admissions policy

For many centres further issues will arise in the admissions policy:

- Local authority children's centres and family centres will most likely only admit through referral of a family by professionals such as a health visitor or social worker. Some may accept self-referrals by parents.
- Workplace day nurseries may only be available to parents who are employed by the funding organisation.
- Community children's centres may operate within a local catchment area. Nursery schools and classes may also give priority to families who live within a given radius of the school.
- Playgroups which are dependent on volunteer support may make admission of children dependent on a promise from parents to join the rota.
- Centres with limited bathroom facilities may insist that children must be reliably toilet trained before they can attend.
- Drop-in facilities such as parent and toddler groups may offer a service that requires parents to stay in the building and continue to take responsibility for their babies or children.
- Crèches may be available only to parents and other carers who use a particular facility, such as a shopping centre or classes in a leisure centre.

An informal policy?

Your centre may work on a very informal basis. Perhaps you explain the work of the centre in conversation with parents and then operate a waiting list when demand outstrips the number of places.

Informal admissions policies may work, but can suffer from two problems:

1 Ensuring consistency between workers when much is dependent on word of mouth.
2 Reassuring parents and other enquirers that the admissions policy is unbiased, when they see nothing to support what they have been told.

It is better practice to have a written policy clearly displayed in your centre which forms part of any leaflets or posters describing the centre's work.

Unacceptable restrictions through admissions policies

Some variety in admissions policies is inevitable given the wide range of early years settings. However, no policy should be worded so it excludes children from particular kinds of families, whether this exclusion is deliberate or unintentional. For instance, a centre could be challenged if there seemed to be no rationale behind choosing the catchment area except to exclude children from the local homeless families' accommodation or an area with many black residents.

You should seek advice from the local early years advisors if your centre is closely associated with a particular religious group. Early years centres, in contrast with groups set up solely for religious instruction, cannot restrict entry to children from families who attend the particular place of worship.

The advisors will want to be reassured that children from other religions, or families with no specific religious beliefs, are made welcome and that other faiths are shown respect.

TO THINK ABOUT

Consider how far your admissions policy is even-handed in practice.

1 How do families find out about your centre?
2 How do you promote the service offered by your centre?
3 Where do you place leaflets or posters? In which publications do you advertise?

If you work in a local authority children's centre or family centre then admission may only be through referral from a social worker or health visitor. In this case, make contact with a different kind of local centre and explore their approach to promoting their own centre.

You will find more about the process of admissions and involvement of parents in Chapter 5.

1.5 Planning and reviewing work

Planning work with children

If your centre is to be of real benefit to the children, then you have to think through in detail the following key questions:

- What do you plan to offer the children in terms of play activities and the daily routine of the centre?
- How will you check that the range of activities is balanced to support children's whole development? How will you adjust your plans for children of different ages and abilities? In a nutshell, in what ways will your plans promote learning for all the children?
- How will you ensure that you notice what children are learning or if children do not seem to be progressing? This question raises issues of observation and useful record keeping.

These practical concerns take you straight to the adults in the nursery and two further sets of questions:

- How will your staff present the activities to children? How should the adults behave towards the children, in order to support their learning? Plans that look good on paper will not benefit children unless workers pay close attention to the children, offer appropriate help and create an encouraging and affectionate atmosphere.
- How will your centre inform and involve parents in their children's learning? Your centre's written policies have to be clear and easily available to parents, but conversation is equally important. For instance, if you explain well, then parents will understand how you are building up the basis for literacy so that 'proper reading and writing' can follow.

An early years curriculum

The ideas underpinning a curriculum for young children are not new. For many years, good practice with young children has been to offer a full range of play activities in order to support children's whole development. Effective early years workers have looked carefully at individual children to see what and how they are learning through their play.

The shift in emphasis with a planned curriculum is to start from the framework of what children could and should be learning. Play activities are then organised with direct links to children's current learning and how they could progress in their whole development. The most effective planning uses the opportunities of the whole centre day, including care routines, and is not restricted to those activities which seem to be more obviously 'educational'.

Vouchers and desirable outcomes

The introduction of the nursery vouchers scheme has brought additional emphasis to how a curriculum should support children in learning through the concept of 'desirable outcomes'. The School Curriculum and Assessment Authority (SCAA) has described the skills, outlook and behaviour that should be the goals in work with children prior to compulsory school. Children vary considerably, so it is expected that some will exceed the goals and others will still be working towards them in primary school.

If you wish to be considered for the receipt of vouchers, your centre will have to publish the details of your curriculum. Inspection will establish how far the quality of provision is appropriate for achieving desirable outcomes in different parts of the curriculum. (Inspectors will not be assessing individual children.)

Reading on . . .

★   The School Curriculum and Assessment Authority (SCAA) has produced booklets for those who work with children in England and leaflets written for parents. You can obtain these by calling the Nursery Education Information Line on 0345 543 345. Similar material is being produced by the Curriculum and Assessment Authority for Wales (01222 375400) and the Scottish Consultative Council on the Curriculum (01382 455053).

Framework for an early years curriculum

This section follows the six key areas for children's learning given in the SCAA material. A few examples are given for each area of learning and this outline could support your more detailed plans. Any early years team should review the curriculum at regular intervals. No programme should be viewed as fixed or beyond constructive criticism.

1 Personal and social development

Encouraging children to be individuals should underpin any curriculum. Your aim is to support children as they learn:

- to develop confidence and a sense of self-worth that is not dependent on undermining other children.
- how to take care of themselves in everyday physical needs;
- to build relationships with adults and children outside the family;
- to develop awareness and concern for the needs of others;
- to play cooperatively with other children.

Activities to support children
Display children's work and acknowledge their effort as well as achievement. Use events and play materials to reflect the cultural backgrounds of families and the broader society. Show and trust children to take on some of their own care. Let them help within the centre routine. Make friends with children and help them to make friends with each other. Set a good example yourself for awareness of others' feelings and needs. Set and explain simple rules for behaviour in your centre. Ensure fair give and take with limited play resources and introduce games that help children to wait their turn or work together.

2 Language and literacy

Opportunities for communication are available throughout the centre day to promote language learning, even for the very youngest who do not yet speak. Important goals are that children:

- become confident with English as a spoken language;
- develop skills of listening and expressing themselves;
- enjoy and appreciate different uses of language;
- learn the basis for writing and reading.

Activities to foster communication
Encourage conversation during any play activity, snack and meal time. Set a good example as an adult: listen, show interest, avoid interruptions. Use songs, rhymes, books and displays. Use variety in these resources to show respect for all the languages of bilingual children. Calm down a very noisy room and create quiet corners. Use story telling as well as books read aloud, drama and resources for imaginative play. Use clear writing within the centre. Use drawing, pattern making and creating books with children. Support children who are ready to start writing or reading.

3   Mathematics

Young children are building the basis to mathematical understanding:

- ideas of shape (two- and three-dimensional), position and size;
- quantity, numbers and their many uses;
- counting and operations of addition and subtraction;
- how to apply simple maths to practical problem solving.

Activities to give practical experience
Construction equipment, drawing and shape making; displays to highlight shape or relative size; books, songs and rhymes; board and card games. Application of maths in sorting out equipment, cooking activities and in trips to the shops; maths games on the computer. Use conversation to give children the correct words to describe what they see and feel. Encourage them to look closely, talk about what they see and draw conclusions.

4   Knowledge and understanding of the world

Within an early years curriculum you are laying the foundations for what will later become the subject areas of history, geography, technology and science. With young children you are exploring:

- the development of an understanding of the past as well as the present;
- awareness of their immediate environment and interest in further afield;
- interest and alertness to the natural world and living things;
- use of materials, tools and equipment for a purpose.

Activities to stimulate curiosity and understanding
Talk with children, answer their questions and search for information together; use scrapbooks, displays and simple observational records. Do projects, e.g. local history or the changing seasons. Observe the wildlife in a local park. Invite parents to talk about their childhood or different countries. Show suitable videos or television programmes. Do gardening and grow indoor plants; make collections and interest tables; do experiments in the water tray, e.g. floating and sinking.

5   Physical development

Children learn too through their physical skills. They can develop interests, a more active and healthy life style and gain in confidence. Help them to:

- develop the larger motor skills of running, climbing, jumping;
- improve skills with fine movements that require careful hand–eye coordination;
- apply physical skills to use tools and materials to make something or solve a problem.

A range of physical activities

Play with outdoor apparatus such as bikes, skipping ropes, bats and balls; for very young children and babies substitute safe indoor equipment and a playful adult. Play indoor and outdoor games which can be children's resources supplemented by adult suggestions. Use construction materials and puzzles; painting, junk and clay modelling, collage and sewing. Develop skills in self care, through help in the nursery routine, dressing up and doll play.

6 Creative development

Creativity is the ability to produce something original. It could be a fresh idea, a tune or something practical such as an embroidered bag. Your curriculum should allow children to:

- develop and follow their imagination, explore possibilities;
- express their feelings and become aware of experience through the senses;
- experiment with different art and craft materials and find satisfaction in the process.

Activities to promote creativity

Imaginative play – music, dance, drama and story telling. Make it easy for children to express their feelings to you; use conversation to explore ideas. Experiment with texture, colour, shape and form through art and craft activities.

Specific plans for individual children or for different age ranges will lead to a choice of appropriate activities. Play opportunities should blend new ideas and variety with familiarity. Children need new, exciting challenges as well as the chance to practise existing skills.

Positive routines for the day

An early years centre without some kind of routine would be a confusing place for children and adults alike. Routines need to be developed and followed both to support the smooth running of a centre and to maximise the chances that the children's days will be enjoyable and help them to learn.

Babies and children feel reassured by knowing what comes next. Young children enjoy being trusted to take part in centre routines. They can extend their skills of self-help during tidying up time or in preparing for snacks or meals. You will need a centre timetable for domestic routines such as meals, toileting and rest, as well as all the different kinds of play activities. However, the routine should never become more important than the children.

Some centres will also have regular visits from other professionals, such as a doctor or speech therapist. Any routine needs some flexibility so that special events can be arranged for children.

TO THINK ABOUT

It is important to manage children's expectations, especially when there is to be a change in routine. In what ways do you prepare children or parents when:

- the centre is going to have visitors, for instance, a group of health visitor students?
- the centre will be shutting for one day for a staff training workshop or for a longer period of time, perhaps over Christmas?
- individual members of staff will be absent on holiday?

 CASE STUDY

In a recent team meeting, workers at Walton Green Family Centre raised two concerns about the daily routine with Maryam, the manager:

- The team has felt it important that meals should be social times for children and adults. However, relaxed lunches have been disrupted since the arrival of the new cook. Workers feel harassed to finish quickly and clear all the plates on to the trolley. Friendly approaches to the cook have been met with, 'You lot don't understand how much I have to get done!'

- Walton Green is the only family centre in the district and many professionals and students express an interest. The team are concerned that there have been too many visitors recently. Unexpected appearances are disturbing children's concentration and worrying some parents.

1 How far do you feel that the team's concerns are reasonable?
2 What steps should Maryam take?
3 Consider any incident that led you to review the routine of your centre.

Planning work with individual children and families

As well as an overall plan for working with the children, centres will need individual plans that focus on the needs of children or their parents. Such plans might not be made in detail for every child and some plans might include a more informal agreement, for example to 'boost Anna's confidence at every opportunity'.

If you work in a local authority children's centre then your group of children is very likely to include many with developmental delays or behaviour that needs a positive focus. Family centre workers will plan specific programmes of work with a whole family and will almost certainly draw up a written agreement with parents that lays out the responsibilities of family and centre. (See also Chapter 6.)

The value of records

It is impossible to plan effectively for individual children and families without informative records. Any centre that has a regular group of children attending should keep some record of individual children's learning. Drop-in centres or parent and child clubs would not keep this kind of record, although workers might well have conversations with parents about the children.

Descriptive records of babies and children should include regular checks on their range of skills in the different areas of development, their interests and behaviour in common situations that arise in the centre. For these records to be as objective as possible, workers should use a prepared record or developmental guide. Any opinions expressed should always be supported by a worker's reasons and a balance should be sought between describing progress and problems.

Reading on . . .

★ Drummond, Mary-Jane, Rouse, Dorothy and Pugh, Gillian 1992: *Making Assessment Work – Values and principles in assessing young children's learning* (National Children's Bureau/NES Arnold).
★ Hobart, Christine and Frankel, Jill 1995: *A Practical Guide to Activities for Young Children* (Stanley Thornes).
★ Lindon, Jennie and Lance 1993: *Caring for the Under-8s: Working to achieve good practice* (Macmillan).
★ Lindon, Jennie 1997: *Working with Young Children* (Hodder and Stoughton).

Reviewing work with children and families

Centres should review both the overall plan for work with children and individual plans for children or families. There are several aspects of an effective reviewing process:

● Part of any plan should be to set a review date on which the plan will be discussed in detail. The aim of the review is to identify progress but consideration also needs to be given to what has not gone well and what could be learned for the future.
● Workers can use their skills of observation to monitor the plans on a continuous basis. Informal records, perhaps a daily diary, can be valuable in noting an activity that children especially enjoyed or how a parent's involvement showed previously unseen talents.
● The opinions of children are equally important to an objective assessment of the work of the centre. Even young children will express a view if they are encouraged and have learned that this adult listens and values children's opinions.
● Parents should be offered a voice in reviews of the overall work of a centre. They will have opinions on the kind of activities offered and the general direction of the work with children. Meetings or conversations with parents can show whether or not the centre's approach is clear to parents and highlight parents' disagreement.
● Part of the review of a plan for an individual child or family will be to consider the goals that were set. How closely have the goals been met? Have they, in fact, been exceeded?

ACTIVITY

Take the opportunity to think in detail about one particular play session in which you have been involved with children. Don't wait for a session that seems to go perfectly; there is much to learn from events that do not unfold as you expected. Ideally, do this activity with a colleague who has also been closely involved in the play session or has been able to observe.

Evaluate the play session by thinking over and answering the following questions:

1   What were the children doing? Never mind how you planned they would use the play materials, what did they actually do?

2   What do you believe that the children were learning? What makes you think that?

3   Did the activity work? From whose point of view – the children's? the workers'?

4   In what way were you involved in the play sessions? What exactly did you do?

5   List at least four things that you believe you have learned from this play session.

This activity is modified from an exercise in Mary Jane Drummond *et al.* (1989) *Working with Children: Developing a curriculum for early years*. National Children's Bureau.

2 Managing an early years centre

This chapter covers:

- the skills of managing an early years centre;
- decision-making and problem-solving;
- writing reports;
- working with other professionals;
- working with a management committee;
- managing change.

2.1 Effective management

Responsibilities of a centre manager

A manager, and in many ways the deputy as well, has four broad bands of responsibility:

- The tasks that have to be done, and done well, if good practice is to be maintained in the centre.
- The individual needs of workers – what they want and feel, both in their short- and long-term professional development.
- How the group of workers is functioning as a team, and the extent to which goals are being set appropriately and achieved.
- Managing the broader context in which the centre operates, including patterns of accountability and the values that shape the work.

These four areas should not be seen as separate. On the contrary, they are best viewed as circles that overlap and intermingle.

As a manager, you need to maintain good working relationships with team members but your role is distinct. You owe loyalty in two directions: to your staff team and to your line management. You have different responsibilities, accountability and more power than workers. Managers who claim, 'I'm just another member of the team' are confused about their role and undervaluing their potential.

Managers have three main parts to their role. You will delegate some tasks but still retain overall responsibility that the job is done well.

- *The flow of information* – You will be responsible for directing the flow of information into the centre as well as internal communications. You will also pass on information and views to your line management, a management committee or meeting of other professionals. You are a key spokesperson for the centre.

An effective manager listens to workers and makes changes accordingly

- *Dealing with people* – You will be responsible for the development and maintenance of good working relationships within the centre (see also Chapters 3 and 4) and between the centre and other parts of the service.
- *Making decisions* – If you insisted on making all decisions alone you would probably anger your staff and lose their loyalty. A good manager consults with the team and weighs up possibilities, but the final responsibility rests with you. Managers have to make hard decisions about the allocation of scarce resources – time, people and money – you cannot please everyone.

TO THINK ABOUT

A manager and senior workers need to show that they value all the individual staff. You demonstrate this through constructive feedback and regular acknowledgement of good work. Early years centres are offering a personal service to children and families. Staff who feel unappreciated are very unlikely to offer full support to families.

Leading or managing?

Management and leadership are two equally important but different parts of the manager's role.

- The tasks of management focus on the immediate and short-term concerns of a centre and are based on past experience of how the centre runs.

Managing relies on accurate information and feedback. The skills are related to guiding and controlling the daily practice of the centre. So management is largely impersonal and objective, for instance what staff should do.

- Leadership focuses on people's wants and aspirations, and on working collectively to achieve a vision of the future. Leadership is therefore motivational and requires looking forward. As a leader, the manager has to maintain a clear perspective on where the team is going and be adaptable to events. The qualities of leadership are especially important when early years centres face change (see section 2.5).

TO THINK ABOUT

Most centre managers are women. Female managers are, of course, a varied group and early years managers experience a different situation from women who are a minority in an organisation. Yet, it is still relevant to consider what it means to be a female manager. In British society the two sexes still face different social pressures and this experience affects choices in style of decision-making or resolving conflict.

These two books have some thought-provoking ideas:

LaRouche, Janice and Ryan, Regina 1985: *Strategies for Women at Work* (Unwin).

Sitterly, Connie 1994: *The Woman Manager: How to develop essential skills of success* (Kogan Page).

See page 62 for a discussion of men in child care and early education.

Good organisation

The manager and the deputy of a centre need to be well organised. You will be helped by good systems, for instance, in finance or record keeping (see Chapter 1) but systems typically only deal with regular and predictable tasks. The manager has to handle whatever happens within the day.

Time and priorities

The key to good management is managing your own time. Spend your time doing those tasks for which you are responsible and not everyone else's.

The many demands of an early years centre can feel overwhelming and an unorganised manager will ricochet from one issue to another. There are techniques for bringing order out of potential chaos:

- Use a diary or a wall chart for forward planning and a daily organiser to keep track of today's work.
- Assign specific times within today or future dates in your diary. Do not mark anything vaguely with a.s.a.p.
- Assign priorities on your daily organiser, rather than an undifferentiated list. Mark your items as 'urgent' or 'important'. If the task is neither of these, then why is it on your list? Complete the urgent items first and transfer any outstanding items to the daily organiser for the following day.
- Consider each item and deal with it appropriately:
  – can or should you refer this on?
  – can you delegate this item?

ACTIVITY

Find out what you are doing with your time. If you feel hard-pressed already, then of course this exercise will take some time! But you will be better organised afterwards, so it is time well spent.

Draw up a time record chart for a full week and split every day into fifteen minute segments. Note down what you are doing in each quarter-hour. Then, at the end of each day, check each activity against one of the columns:

1   Tick this column if you did the right thing at the right time.
2   This is for when you did the right thing but at the wrong time. You can see now that this task would have been better completed earlier or left until later.
3   You did the wrong thing. This did not have to be done at all or not by you.

At the end of your week analyse your daily charts.

1   Are you losing time searching for items that have not been properly filed? Are you doing tasks

Time record chart		Date:		
Time	What I did	1	2	3
8.00				
8.15				
8.40				
8.45				
9.00				
And so on....				

yourself that could be delegated? Are you mis-timing your tasks? Are you delayed by other workers' tardiness?
2   Note four ways in which you could improve your time management. Look at the ideas in this section.

– do you have to do something? If so, what, how and when?
– do you need more information? If so, what and from whom?
– is it appropriate to defer a decision? If so, write a note in your diary.
– do you need to make a note, but no further action?

Careful time management means that you avoid panics. For instance, because you have assigned an hour today to write a difficult report, you are not chased next week by 'Where's that report you promised?'

You should assign some time simply to being visible about the centre: this behaviour has been called 'managing by wandering around'. If you regularly spend some time with staff and groups of children, this pattern will be seen as normal. However, if you rarely emerge from the office, then your staff will wonder 'What's she up to?' when you do appear in the room.

Delegation

The rule is to delegate to the most junior person who can do the task passably well. Centre managers will often delegate to their deputies, who should be given the opportunity to learn management skills. Deputies should be clear about what they can delegate in their turn.

The process of delegation is more than 'Here, you do this'. Experienced workers need to be able to explain a task well and allow staff to ask questions. (See also 'Coaching' on page 90.) Allow staff time to learn their new responsibilities and do not judge them harshly when they could not be expected to be as confident or efficient at this task as you.

Hard-pressed senior workers often say, 'It's quicker if I do it myself'. This judgement may be true in the short term but is not a good use of time in the longer term. Doing a ten-minute job yourself every week is not as effective as spending thirty minutes to brief a worker to take over the task. Attention

ACTIVITY

Save your daily organiser lists in a folder and check them after a couple of weeks.

1   Are there any items that you keep transferring from day to day? What is holding you back from tackling this particular task? Should you delegate it?
2   Review those tasks which you designate as 'urgent' rather than 'important'. Is there a pattern? Does this pattern make sense if you consider the objectives of your centre?

Delegation by expertise

Some decisions are best taken by a worker with special experience or a sub-group set up for this purpose. For instance, Wai has the most relevant experience to run the group for Vietnamese refugee families. She discusses her plans with the manager but makes most of the daily decisions.

Majority vote

When a staff group fails to reach an agreement, decisions may be taken by a vote. This approach leaves some dissenters but is fine for minor issues such as 'What colour shall we paint the staff room?'

Seeking consensus

Group decision by consensus is time-consuming since it requires group discussion in which everyone participates and a decision is reached that is acceptable to everyone. Seeking consensus is worth the effort for decisions that will have serious impact on the running of the centre. Some changes will not work without individual commitment and this will not be achieved without consensus.

Decision-making in groups

A team meeting should, in theory, be the best way to resolve practice issues that affect everyone. Yet many people have bad experiences of trying to reach decisions or to resolve problems through group discussion.

Research on groups has shown the best approach to be a three-step process:

1 Firstly, the group needs to explore what exactly is the issue that requires a decision. It is crucial to define what is, and what is not, the problem. This is an information-gathering phase.
2 Once the problem has been defined, group members should put their energy and ideas into an analysis of the possible alternatives to resolving the issue. (In time this should be about the middle of the meeting.)
3 Finally, the group considers which alternative is, on balance, the best option to take forward. Towards the end of the meeting they decide what needs to be done, by whom, and by when.

Observational research of many groups has shown that, without an informed and firm leader, few groups follow this logical pattern. The more usual muddle is illustrated by the case study that follows.

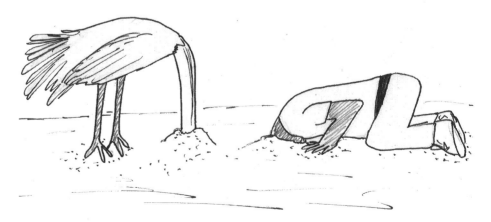

Ignoring problems does not make them disappear

CASE STUDY

The Gables Community Nursery met problems in implementing an anti-sexist approach to work with the children. (See also the case study on page 5.) Keith, the manager, called a special team meeting to discuss the issues.

Keith has been studying problem-solving on his management course and the team agreed for him to set up video equipment to record the meeting. Later, everyone felt that the meeting had not helped to sort out the issues, so they opted to watch the video. Once everyone stopped squirming, they began to see what went awry.

- They had next to no discussion of 'What exactly is the problem we are facing here?' Instead there was an energetic flurry as everyone put forward his or her pet solution. They hear themselves saying, 'What we should do is rewrite the policies.' 'No, no. That's no use. We should have a full parents' meeting.' And then 'What's the point of that?' and so on.

- Competition over solutions decreased but did not fade completely, as workers realised that they disagreed on how policies were entangled in the issue. Nobody really acknowledged the confusion and worry within the team about the clash of values, policies and views of parents. Keith tried to bring the team back to addressing the nature of the problem but also got caught up in the many side issues.

- Discussion of alternatives was confused with pet solutions. However, nobody really accepted that there might not be an answer that would please everyone – workers and parents.

- By the end of the meeting a sense of panic set in: 'We have to sort out what we are going to do!' But everyone watching the tape admits that they are confused about what, if anything, was decided.

The team decide to hold another meeting, with a strong agenda to use the three steps of problem-solving.

1 Does this sound familiar to you? Consider revisiting a situation that arose in your own team meetings by using the logical steps in decision-making and problem-solving.

2 Think of any meeting you have attended recently. There are a range of different kinds listed on page 70. To what extent were the logical steps followed? What happens if there is a 'free for all'?

2.4 Working with other professionals

Working with a management committee
Patterns of accountability

All early years centres are accountable to some other body.

- Managers of private nurseries have to communicate with the owner, even if that person gives them a great deal of freedom to run the nursery.
- Managers of local authority centres have line managers within social services and may also report to users' committees.
- In a nursery or reception class, you will be accountable to the teaching staff, who are, in turn, accountable to their line management and to the board of school governors.
- Community nurseries and playgroups may be run by managers who are responsible to a management committee.

This section covers the working relationship with a management committee, but many points are equally relevant if you report to any group.

Role and responsibilities

All workers, including the manager, need clear roles and responsibilities in work with the management committee. Such committees vary in how they work, for instance, in the level of formality of their meetings or in how active a role is taken by committee members in the details of centre life.

Workers will be responsible for the daily running of the centre in the context of policies set by the committee. The committee will most likely interview and appoint workers and should provide all workers with contracts of employment and job descriptions. These should clarify the boundaries of the manager's role in the centre and make clear how you should report to and consult the management committee.

The committee itself has to be set up with clear boundaries. There should be a constitution which determines details such as:

- the frequency of meetings;
- how finance is handled;
- how the committee is to be made up;
- how new members are to be found.

Any management committee should have a leader who will chair meetings. The leader may be the primary contact for the centre manager or for parents who wish to go beyond the centre staff. There should also be a secretary responsible for any records and a treasurer who will deal with the finances.

The manager will probably undertake most of the liaison with the committee, although other workers might be involved, for example, to present special reports. All staff would have contact when committee members visit the centre. The manager is responsible for keeping the committee fully informed about the running of the centre.

- The committee will want to be assured that policies are being put into practice. Managers will have to report promptly on any difficulties or potential clashes between different policy requirements.
- The committee will not want a blow-by-blow account of every detail, but they are likely to want written plans outlining the pattern of work with

the children in full-day or sessional facilities. They may also want to hear fairly detailed plans for any special events within the centre.

- The committee will make decisions about the budget and will look to the manager for a realistic forecast of costs and income.
- The committee will take an active role in the complaints procedure for centre users, grievance procedures for workers and in disciplinary action. The chair will expect a manager to keep him or her fully informed if any of these procedures are likely to be implemented, for instance, if a parent is seriously dissatisfied and threatening to make a formal complaint. Written reports will be part of the process.
- You need to be clear what the committee asks you to do within the centre. It is far better to ask for clarification than to carry on with uncertainty or wrong assumptions. Confusions would not necessarily be referred to the full committee. You should be able to consult the chair, especially on those issues where boundaries of confidentiality have to be determined.

You encourage children to work well together – you may sometimes have to work at good relationships with other professionals

Issues relevant to working with a management committee are discussed in other sections of the book:

- Policies in an early years centre – section 1.1.
- Budgets and financial issues – section 1.3.
- Plans in the work with children – section 1.5.
- Effective meetings – section 3.4.
- Disciplinary procedures – section 4.4.
- Complaints procedures – section 5.3.

Reading on . . .

★ 1995: *Playgroup Committees and Constitutions* (Pre-school Learning Alliance). This booklet is useful for any early years centre.

Working with local services

Any centre has to have good external communications. Early years centres vary in their particular blend of care and education but all need to have good working relationships with local services. In particular:

- statutory education, including special needs provision;
- health services for children and families;
- specialist areas such as psychological services, speech therapy and physiotherapy;
- social services, including child protection;
- the local police.

You should have information about the local services in a regularly updated folder. Write a name and telephone number for as many services as possible.

No centre could expect to cover all eventualities and it is wise to seek additional support with the full involvement of children's parents. Bear in mind that different services do not work in the same ways, so you should check whether another professional takes a similar approach to your centre, for example, on confidentiality or partnership with parents. You need to establish ground rules together. Flexibility will be important in establishing good working relationships, but should not lead to actions that are contrary to the values and policies of the centre.

In some cases, specialist support for children may be offered by other professionals who visit the centre. Children should not be referred or seen without their parents' explicit permission. It is good practice for parents to be present for any kind of special assessment or help.

 CASE STUDY

For the last two years Mount Park Children's Centre has sent descriptive reports of the children to their primary school, with the aim of providing continuity in children's care. These reports were honest yet written carefully to highlight children's real progress. The reports were always discussed with the parents, who sometimes added their own comments.

Leela, the manager, had been disappointed that only two of the four local primary school heads had ever made contact over the reports. She has also been made uneasy by a conversation with one parent whose older child has started at school. This parent had been told by a reception teacher that she did not usually want reports from pre-school centres but that it was useful with 'problem children like yours'. The assumption seemed to be that all children from a local authority centre would prove to be difficult in school.

1. What do you judge are the issues that have to be weighed up in sending reports of children to their next stage? What are the positive sides to sending a written report and what are the potential risks?

2. How would you proceed now, if you were Leela?

Working with inspection services

The Children Act 1989 required that most day-care facilities for under-eights be registered and inspected on an annual basis. Some centres were already accountable to their line management or to the funding organisation, but thorough checking by external inspectors was a new experience. With the introduction of nursery vouchers, centres who wish to be eligible will have to be checked by Department for Education and Employment (DfEE) inspectors (see also section 1.5).

There are better ways to plan ahead

Even workers in centres with good practice can feel uneasy about the prospect of being judged. You may find the experience less uncomfortable with subsequent inspections as you understand exactly what the process entails. The manager and senior workers need to encourage the whole team to look constructively at inspection. Any inspection team should support quality in work by:

- providing detailed guidelines on what centres are expected to provide for children and families. All local authorities should have published standards for day and sessional care inspected under the Children Act. The DfEE has published booklets about desirable outcomes for an early years curriculum;
- giving constructive feedback in conversation and a written report. You should be complimented on high standards achieved in your practice as well as directed to areas that should be improved;
- giving any requests for change in sufficient detail that you can understand what is wanted. There should also be a time scale.

Reading on . . .

For working with inspection services try:

★ Cowley, Liz 1993: *Registration and Inspection of Day Care for Young Children* (National Children's Bureau).

★ The Office for Standards in Education 1995: *The Ofsted Handbook: Guidance on the inspection of nursery and primary schools* (HMSO).

For setting up local professional networks try:

★ 1991: *Setting Up an Early Years Forum: A step-by-step guide* (The National Early Years Network).

2.5 Managing change

The experience of change
Different types of change

Any job involves some level of change but the changes are not always substantial. There are three types of change in work situations.

Routine

There will be regular, minor changes and adjustments in work practices and procedures. In an early years centre you will sometimes be buying in new equipment, you may make small changes to the staff shift system and sometimes you will have temporary staff. Some routine changes are an inevitable part of the work and most people accept and welcome the variety. Children develop and their individual needs change during their time with you. There will always be some turnover of children and parents, greater in some centres than in others.

Improvement

A second type of change involves more extensive adjustments to current policies and practices. You are not introducing entirely new ways of working but are reviewing, enhancing and perhaps correcting your existing ways. People are more likely to resist this kind of change on the grounds that, 'It's worked fine this way so far, so why change it?' Much depends on the extent to which workers believe that reviewing practice is the professional approach.

Innovation

Innovative changes are designed to bring in new ways of working and may replace some of the previous practices. Such changes are introduced in order to make the service responsive to the future needs of users. This type of change can make a significant difference in how a centre is organised and how workers are expected to behave.

   The pressures towards change may come from a management committee or the funding organisation of the centre. Alternatively, the stimulus may be internal, for instance, when new workers bring in different ideas or existing workers are enthused by a training course.

Recent change for early years centres

Inspection

Most centres will now experience the process of inspection – either from the local authority under the Children Act 1989 or from OFSTED if they are within the education sector.

Standards and quality

There has been an emphasis on quality and on improvements beyond the basic minimum. Each centre will have an individual feel but should not be allowed to follow a direction determined only by the manager, owner or funding body. The Children Act and supporting guidance introduced the concept of minimum standards in all aspects of the work. The issue of quality assurance now arises for centres eligible for nursery vouchers.

Reviews of good practice

Substantial reviews of good practice have led to rethinking policies and practice. Some key areas have been:

- equal opportunities on race, gender and disability. A major theme has been that early years centres should take an active approach in promoting equal opportunities and in counteracting prejudice and discrimination. Vague good intentions are insufficient;
- an early years curriculum (EYC) approach. This has developed as a response to the changes of the National Curriculum for older children. EYC can have much in common with a planned approach to learning through play;
- partnership with parents. This has signalled a shift towards a more equal relationship with parents and other carers, rather than offering involvement mainly on a centre's terms. Reassessment of local authority day care has led many day nurseries to move into family work, even if they have not become family centres entirely;
- the approach to child protection. This has become more detailed and organised. With the acceptance that some parents may harm their own children has come the professional responsibility for prevention and protection;
- the children's rights movement. This has been supported by the UN Convention on the Rights of the Child. The movement emphasises children's perspective and their right to a voice. In a view shared with the Children Act, parents are seen as having responsibilities towards children and young people rather than absolute rights over them.

For some early years centres reviews of good practice have given workers a clearer framework to guide what was already current practice. For other centres, such a review could be a significant change since the implications required a substantial overhaul in ways of working.

Structural changes

Those centres within local authorities or the education sector have often been through institutional reorganisation, sometimes more than once. Centres may have become the responsibility of a different department with new line management. Such changes can also affect practice in decision-making, finance and reporting.

Individuals and change

Attempts to bring about change in the workplace are rarely successful unless the *process* of managing change is understood and followed. Certainly, effective change will not be managed through a single route. For instance, insisting that all workers attend a general race awareness course will probably not improve practice unless there is also detailed discussion on how to apply the ideas to the work with children and parents.

A practical reminder is to be aware that:

- it is easier to change the situation than to change a person's behaviour;
- it is easier to change behaviour than to change someone's attitudes;
- it is easier to change attitudes than to change the individual's personal make-up.

Anyone involved in the change process needs to remain realistic and to begin with attempts at change that have a reasonable chance of success.

EXAMPLE

Naomi was very wary in any conversation with parents and critical of their standards in comparison with her own expertise. The situation at Salmon Lane Private Nursery changed when Debbie, the manager, organised regular meetings for parents to discuss their children's progress.

Naomi had no choice but to take part in these meetings and, with Debbie also present, she bit back some of her more dismissive remarks. The setting of the meeting forced her to listen more to parents and she grudgingly admitted that some of them cared more about their children than she had believed. The consequence was that Naomi was more ready, at least with some parents, to talk informally at the end of the day.

Debbie realised that Naomi's hostility to parents was probably part of her defensive approach to life. Naomi's personal outlook would be more difficult to tackle and might not lie within Debbie's responsibilities.

- A realistic approach can be to regard workers' attitudes as their own business until these emerge through their behaviour as poor practice. Consider circumstances in your own centre when it was, or could be, most practical to look at how you could change the working situation for an individual rather than trying first to change attitudes.

Different kinds of change

Individual change in early years practice may require adjustments in any, and sometimes all, of the following areas:

Behavioural – changing what people do or how they do it
Workers may need to learn new skills, but sometimes the change requires that they use skills they already possess but do not yet apply in this context.

For instance, the development of family work in a centre may mean that all workers should be trained in basic counselling skills, and some in family therapy or group work. On the other hand, a move towards greater partnership in a centre might require workers to apply their existing skills of communication more frequently in two-way exchanges with parents.

Psychological
Workers may have to face change in their personal values and assumptions. Their attitudes may be challenged and they may be expected to justify, and perhaps change, their opinions. For example, integrating children with disabilities can mean that workers need to look carefully at their own attitudes and the source of their beliefs, as well as their behaviour.

Social
Change may also require adjustments in working relationships, both inside and outside the centre. The introduction of a key worker system, for instance, would necessitate some changes in the pattern of relationships with colleagues, parents and children. The establishment of an Early Years Forum for support and development in local centres would introduce a new set of relationships between centres and other early years professionals.

Cognitive
Some changes might mean that workers need to extend their knowledge. Effective application of equal opportunities on race, culture or religion includes psychological changes but also requires a broader base of information.

Individual reactions

Change, or even the prospect of change, is experienced differently by everyone. As a manager or a senior worker you will need to be aware of the range of reactions to change within the staff group. If you are prepared to reflect on your own feelings and experiences, you will also gain some insight into your own responses to change in the work. Essentially, to help change to be successful everyone needs to find some *personal* benefit in making the change.

Feelings of security

Change – even minor change – can disturb people who do not feel secure or confident. You will be more able to put workers at ease about change if you understand how the prospect unsettles them. Even workers who are fairly confident about facing change can feel threatened if the process is badly handled.

Individuals may also be apprehensive about specific parts of a change process. Will they have to work closely with the one member of the team whom they dislike? Is their job or the existence of the entire centre under threat? If so, resistance to change is likely to be high.

The group beliefs and values

The prevailing feelings of a staff group or local network can shape the reactions to change of individuals. Staff will react negatively to proposed changes if the group's sub-culture is, 'We've done it this way for ten years. Who are you to tell us we're all wrong!' Another staff group might be open to possibilities because they share the outlook that, 'We want our work to develop. It's good to try new ideas.'

Trust

Trust is very important for good team working (see page 56) and the feeling is equally central when workers are assessing a proposal for change. Do the workers in a centre trust the manager and senior staff, since these people will be introducing a change? Do centre staff trust the line management, the department or organisation that is ultimately in charge? Proposals for change will be less well received if workers doubt that the line management understands the real work of the centre or respects their skills.

Previous experience and habit

Any change is interpreted through past experience with this centre or in previous jobs. Historical experience can either help or hinder the change process.

For instance, an early years team may recall the support and careful explanation that helped the shift to more partnership with parents. The team is still wary about what this new early years curriculum approach means for them, but they are prepared to listen and see what is involved. Another staff group may feel cynical and disheartened because they have struggled through a whole series of changes with little explanation or support. Their reaction to yet another change is, 'Here we go again. Another flavour of the month!' They do not see the point, so find it hard to grasp any personal benefit to them.

Workers with bad experiences from other centres can bring negative reactions into a team whose feelings are mainly positive. Senior workers need to move swiftly to counteract dismissive comments like, 'We tried this equal opps stuff in my old nursery. Waste of time; it never worked!' The disillusioned worker may help this team not to repeat mistakes but must not be allowed to dismiss a whole area of good practice without challenge.

How to manage change

A great deal depends on *how* change is introduced. Sensitive handling can calm the worries of individuals and optimise the positive consequences. As manager, you may guide your team through the change. However, an awareness of the steps may also enable you to mediate change when some parts of the process are the responsibility of others. You will be confident to ask questions or push for discussions, knowing that the change process will be ineffective without understanding, information and commitment.

Steps towards change

Even major changes are sometimes pushed through on the pretext of, 'Just do it!' but the end results are unlikely to be positive. Constructive change moves through a series of steps, similar to those in decision-making and problem-solving (see also page 34).

1 *'We need to make a change'*
The process starts with the recognition of the need for change. There is a gap between what is currently happening and what needs to happen. A sense of pressure towards change can come from different sources. Perhaps a series of embarrassing mistakes have highlighted faults in the nursery's accounting system; or the management committee of a playgroup may urge staff to review how children with disabilities are integrated into play activities.

The next two steps are essential for creating the proper climate for change.

2 *'What are the issues here?'*
You now need to discuss the gap in practice that makes you, or someone else, certain that some change is necessary. You need to talk through *all* the issues and to describe the problem(s) *before* considering any solutions.

For instance, there could be a meeting, perhaps several, between the management committee and the whole playgroup staff to explore in detail the gap that the committee members see between current practice and what would be good practice for children with disabilities. Such a meeting should highlight good current practice as well as the improvements deemed necessary.

3 *'What do we want to achieve?'*
The next step in any useful discussion is what would be the desired end results of this change. If you were successful in making this change, what would you have achieved in the centre? What would be happening and in what way, that was not happening before? This step may precede step 2, since steps 1–3 are all about *what* needs to change.

4 *'How might we bring about this change?'*
A thorough discussion at steps 2 and 3 will mean that you can now have a properly focused exploration of the possible ways to approach and bring about this change. Step 4 and subsequent steps focus on *how* the change will be achieved.

For instance, there might be several possible ways of overhauling the nursery's system of accounts and each possibility needs to be discussed. A premature leap for a single solution, such as, 'Let's put it all on computer, then it'll print out everything', might not solve the central problem. Perhaps the manual system is in a mess because nobody has overall responsibility for entering the different transactions.

5 'What would be the best way forward?'

You should now reach a decision on what would be the best approach to bringing about the change. It is possible that the strategy will involve several elements in order to achieve the desired end results.

For example, the chair of the management committee and the playgroup manager might plan a Saturday workshop for the whole staff group, to which they invite two workers from the local special opportunities adventure playground. The aim is to produce definite plans on how to make the playgroup more accessible and welcoming to children with disabilities. Fund-raising possibilities for special equipment are to be explored and dates set for further staff meetings to discuss progress. One worker is to be sent on a relevant training course, with the intention that she reports back in detail to the whole staff group.

6 Implementing the change

Typically, the process of change takes longer and has more setbacks than people anticipate. Even with a motivated and enthusiastic staff group, someone has to be responsible for monitoring how the change is progressing.

Managers might create time in a staff meeting, or plan a separate discussion, to talk through in detail what is working smoothly and any unexpected difficulties that have to be resolved. Sometimes, a plan might have to be modified and workers need clear explanations and encouragement from senior staff. Supervision may be the best time to address individual reservations or resistance.

A staff group needs to integrate any change into their way of working and feel happy that the new ways have now stabilised. Time has to be assigned for discussion and review. A team will be very unsettled if another major change follows before the previous one has been properly worked through into daily practice.

Partnership with parents

In any change, attention should be given to keeping parents informed. You should warn parents of changes and explain the reasons. In the early stages of a major change, it may be best to stress that you are all 'discussing the possibilities'. Parents can become confused and irritated if they are given a series of interim plans that are not later put into practice.

A staff group should discuss how a change will be introduced and explained to parents. It is inappropriate to share workers' worries or frustrations about the change; these should be discussed within the team.

The main vehicles for change

There are five basic routes to change within any organisation and the process of change may draw from all of them. None is particularly neat or easy and all need good communication with staff so that they understand and can ask about what the change means for them.

1 Training and development

You may decide to send some workers on training courses. Relevant courses or workshops can provide the knowledge and skills necessary to make the kind of changes described on page 44. Training courses will not do all the work of implementing change. A mis-chosen or poorly run course may have a negative result and promote opposition to the change.

Workers will also have opportunities to learn within the daily practice. Staff can continue to develop skills through coaching and the supervision system (see Chapter 4).

2 Team building
Attempts to change practice are likely to fade away or take an unwanted side route without good team work (see Chapter 3).

3 Structure and strategy
Change may start or be supported by changes to the organisational structure, either within the centre itself or in how the centre relates to the organisation of which it is a part. Centres may be given a written statement about the new strategy or policies that have to be introduced or adjusted (see section 1.1 for policies and procedures). However well written, a policy will not bring about change on its own, but a clear statement of purpose, and of roles and responsibilities helps a team to focus on the new key tasks.

Workers need to understand exactly what the change means for their daily practice. They need encouragement and accurate, constructive feedback on

---

 CASE STUDY

Mount Park is a local authority children's centre. A year ago the new line manager started to talk about introducing an early years curriculum approach into the centre. Most of the staff group found the phrase disconcerting and the centre grapevine started to buzz.

Leela, the manager, swiftly picked up on anxieties in the team. These included:

- But we're not a school and we're not teachers.
- But we've got under-3s – you don't have a curriculum for them.
- Are you saying that we've been doing it all wrong up to now?
- First this curriculum thing, then it'll be testing the children!

Some staff were less anxious than others, but even the positive ones were concerned about what this change meant for the centre and their own work.

Leela made a date in the near future for the line manager, Vicky, to talk with the whole staff group. In preparation, Leela encouraged individual workers to be ready to voice their questions and concerns. The meeting went well and Vicky was positive about the centre's work. She reassured the team that much of what they were already doing with the children – through themes and planning a play programme – would adapt easily for the EYC approach. Vicky brought a report from work in her previous authority and a wall chart on the topic.

Vicky seemed to believe that this single meeting would be enough for the centre to go ahead with the change. Leela disagreed, seeing the meeting as just a first step, and made a separate appointment to talk with Vicky. From this second meeting and discussion within staff meetings, a plan developed.

Leela and Jack made arrangements to visit two centres in Vicky's previous authority. A date was then set for a full-day workshop for the whole team and letters went out to give parents plenty of warning of the closure day. During planning meetings for each room in the centre, staff began to consider a whole curriculum approach in the play programme. The room discussions were very positive in showing most workers what Vicky had said, i.e. that their approach was already in the direction of EYC.

Leela spent time with Harriet, the one worker who continued to object, but failed to reduce her hostility to EYC. Leela has recognised that Harriet is resistant to any change in her practice. She still complains about the shift from a more traditional day nursery which happened eight years ago.

Leela was now worried that Harriet might drain the enthusiasm of the team, and there are some signs that she has stirred up parents' worries. Leela made a note to discuss this serious concern with Vicky at their next meeting and to consider ways to minimise the effects of Harriet's negative views.

Question
Consider a relatively major change that has been made in your centre in recent years.
a) In your opinion, which parts of the process were well handled?
b) With hindsight, what might you have done differently?
c) In any staff group some workers will be more positive than others. How did you manage the variety in attitudes?

what they do. Workers whose practice is not in line with the change need a clear message, with support, about how they are expected to respond to the change. It will be important for the whole team that the manager recognises and deals with staff whose practice does not change.

4 Patterns of reward and encouragement
Change is also effected by positive consequences for people who work in line with the change. In early years centres this is very unlikely to be financial reward. The positives will be through recognition and appreciation and perhaps the occasional party celebration. Senior workers are responsible for acknowledging the efforts and progress made, however slow this may sometimes seem to be.

5 Values in the service and centre
Attention may need to be paid to values and how a change can require a re-assessment of the values held by a team or the whole local early years service.

Supporting a positive outlook on change

People tend to resist change if they feel either incapable of dealing with the change or they cannot see that any benefits are likely to result. As someone responsible for bringing about change, you need to support your team in seeing the benefits without denying their realistic concerns. You may be communicating some, or most, of the following points:

- Change does not mean your previous practice was wrong. Professional practice continues to change; the willingness to review and continue to learn is part of good practice. Some staff groups, and some individuals, may be especially vulnerable to believing that change is an explicit criticism of them or their work. Sometimes this is true, but not typically.
- Just because you have run a centre in a particular way for many years is not proof that this way is right, but it does not make it wrong either. New ideas should not be blithely accepted on a wave of enthusiasm. The implications should be carefully explored and new ideas questioned in a constructive way: 'What exactly is involved?', 'Where would this lead us?' or 'What are the reasons (or evidence) for this change?'
- Change within early years practice is inevitable as society evolves. It will not be a once-only experience. Discussions about good practice and standards will continue and there will be new legislation and further research. You may need to dissuade your staff group from believing, 'So, once we make this change, we'll be left alone'.
- All early years teams need to use workers' experience positively. Previous experience is a valuable source of information and a way to understanding new ideas and approaches, perhaps to test their practicality. However, remarks such as, 'When you've been doing the job as long as I have, then you'll understand' deserve to be challenged and the speaker invited to share the results of experience – not use the years in order to dismiss others.
- Dealing with change is not all logical. You will help if you allow the expression of feelings within your team. Giving up old ways is often painful. If you recognise and respect these feelings (in yourself as well) you have taken an important step in dealing positively with emotions.

In summary . . .

As an agent of change, it will certainly help if you:

- let the angry confront you;
- hear what the arrogant have to say, without being pushed around by them;
- provide a safe place in which the hurt, the tense and the anxious can open up;
- fire enthusiasm in the bored and disillusioned;
- satisfy the sceptical;
- explain carefully and respectfully to the confused.

Modified from Ruth Carter and others *Systems, Management and Change* (Harper and Row, 1984).

Change is an inevitable part of your work. The main mistake in handling change is usually to stress the advantages to parents or children (or to line management) without showing the benefits to staff, or recognising that staff concerns are real and legitimate. Removing the barriers to change is often the most productive way to support progress in the centre. Offering workers some choices also helps to build commitment. If the goals of the change cannot be modified, then consider if some freedom can be offered to staff in how the goals are achieved.

Reading on . . .

★ Cowley, Liz (ed.) 1995: *Managing to Change: Training materials for staff in day care centres for young children* (National Children's Bureau). This set of four training modules supports staff groups in changing their practice.
★ Hussey, D.E. 1995: *How to Manage Organisational Change* (Kogan Page).
★ Kids' Clubs Network 1996: *Aiming High: Quality assurance scheme for out-of-school clubs*.

3 Developing effective teamwork

This chapter covers:

- building a team;
- organising a team;
- good communication within teams;
- planning and running meetings.

3.1 Building an early years team

What is a team?

Early years workers will need to establish and maintain good communication with a network of professionals but will not work closely with all these people. Effective work in the centre, on the other hand, requires that individual staff recognise that they are members of a team.

Working as a team does not mean that everyone has the same tasks, nor are they expected to carry out their work in an identical way. Teamwork gives scope for individual style and interests. However, individuality is expressed through a shared commitment to a common cause. Individual workers within a team are *interdependent*; what one individual does in his or her work will affect other team members.

This quality of interdependence is positive when everyone remains aware of how their areas of responsibility merge with those of their colleagues. If a few workers behave as if their actions are their own business, a staff group will realise the negative consequence of interdependence. Perhaps one worker has an offhand approach to parents. Her actions may irritate or distress the individual parents and her behaviour is likely to rebound on colleagues. They will experience the backlash of the parents' feelings, including perhaps a generalised belief that, 'Nobody respects parents around here!'

Team building
Enthusiasm for a shared vision

Individuals can work together as a team when they are enthusiastic about what they are doing and feel that the work matters. With a shared understanding of priorities, individuals pull in the same direction. A shared commitment to 'this is why we're here' can also provide a sense of purpose to support teams through frustrating times in the work.

ACTIVITY

You can use these two suggestions to guide your personal thoughts. However, the exercise will be more useful if you involve colleagues.

- Over the last twelve months in your centre, what are the tasks or achievements about which you feel excited or proud. Select five examples.
- Imagine that the local newspaper has shown interest in your centre, but they are only going to write a short article. The reporter asks you to sum up 'what your centre is really all about'. Draft, in no more than 20–25 words, a statement that answers the question, 'What are we here for?'

1 Are there common features running through your work on the two suggestions? If yes, what is the theme? If no, should there be some theme?

2 How similar to those of your colleagues are your answers and ideas?

Commitment to shared values and policies

When you put your team's values into words, you are making a statement about what you *believe* should underpin all aspects of your daily practice. Unless existing team members are clear about values, for instance about equal opportunities or the importance of partnership with parents, you are unlikely to be able to communicate those values clearly to other people.

The values of your centre should be reflected in detailed policies that guide daily practice. A written policy (see section 1.1) demonstrates the commitment of your team and it can support clearer communication over issues that are open to misunderstanding, or to potential disagreement. Values focus on deeply held beliefs and very much reflect *how* work is done at the centre.

 CASE STUDY

For three years, Walton Green Family Centre had hardly any changes in staff. Then, over a period of 12 months, three workers left. Their replacements are experienced, but previously worked in playgroups and nurseries. They are committed to partnership with parents, but are having to adjust to the daily presence of some parents with their children.

A key value for Walton Green has been '*responsiveness and flexibility to the needs of parents*'. Maryam, the manager, and Andrew, her deputy, meet to discuss issues that arose in recent supervision sessions with the new staff. Each worker has faced dilemmas over what flexibility meant in action.

For example, Anouska had felt uncertain when Harry's father said he needed his son's hours to be extended – should she just agree or consult Maryam first? Sergio had been confident to step in when Ella hit her daughter, but he wanted to discuss other incidents when he had been less sure of the boundaries for parents' wishes or preferences.

Maryam and Andrew realise that they had assumed the meaning of the key value was obvious. They discuss how to move forward now.

1 How might Maryam and Andrew best use their own experience and that of the other staff who have been at the centre for some years?

2 Can you recall experiences in your own centre when you, or colleagues, assumed wrongly that the meaning of a key value (or some other aspect of practice) was 'obvious' or 'just common sense'? What did you learn?

Setting workable goals

Shared values come alive because you set goals in your work that are firmly grounded in those values. Part of the process of team building emerges through everyone's commitment to setting workable goals. Such an approach is in contrast to a centre run on the basis that individual workers develop their practice whatever way makes sense to them. In contrast with the *how* of values, goals define end results: what *will* be achieved.

Goals applicable to all team members would be developed from centre policies, for example, integrating children with disabilities into the full play programme. Workers who run a group room, or who are responsible for a regular parents' group, need to develop the particular goals relevant to their work. These goals must be compatible with the goals of the whole centre.

In order for goals to be really useful they need to have particular qualities, which are described below. (If you like memory aids, then SMARTI will help you to remember the points.) Although this chapter focuses on team working, the qualities of a useful goal are just as relevant to planning work with children or parents.

Specific

Goals should make a clear statement about the detail of 'what we are going to do'. Details are important whether you are setting a goal for a programme of work for the whole centre, in your work with an individual child, or in your own learning as a worker. Performance should be the focus – the results and not the effort.

Measurable

A goal cannot be measured unless you can observe whether you have achieved it, or how well you have progressed towards the goal. You do not need complex systems of measurement but make sure that all goals are set in such a way that you, or colleagues, would be able to judge through observation whether the goal had been reached.

Achievable

For everyone's sake, it must be possible to achieve the goals that you have set. Workers, or parents involved in goals for their children, can be very disheartened if they are striving to achieve goals that are too tough.

Agreed goals for the centre still leave plenty of scope for an individual approach

Useful goals are achievable but they are not improved by adding escape clauses, such as 'as far as we can' or 'so long as nothing goes wrong'. The focus has to be on doing. Children or parents benefit from achieving a goal that has been set – not from efforts or good intentions that did not succeed.

TO THINK ABOUT

Read through the goals for children or work with parents that are being set in your centre. Do they include cautious phrases? What is the reaction – your own feelings, or the reaction in the team if you are the manager – if you work to rephrase the goals? If there is reluctance, then think over these two points:

1   If an individual, or most of the centre team, is trying to hedge a goal with 'ifs', 'buts' and 'maybes', then that goal needs further discussion. Are you trying to set a goal in an area of your work which is out of your direct influence? Or is the time frame that you are setting too ambitious?
2   When there is resistance to setting goals in most areas of work, staff may be anxious about being seen to fail. This concern about how mistakes are handled should be tackled as an issue in its own right.

Realistic

It has to be possible to achieve the goals in the relatively near future. Goals might require some extra effort, but should not demand that all other responsibilities in your work are sacrificed.

With more enthusiasm than realism, goals can be set that are impractical. Perhaps the goal is too ambitious – given a child's current development or limits to the centre's resources. Workers also need to realise that some aspects of children's, or parents', lives are not within their control.

Additionally, you cannot work towards goals unless they are based on freedom of action. It is no use setting goals which depend on the behaviour or attitudes of other people; you cannot control these and your ability to influence may be limited.

Time-bound

Goals do not make much sense unless you specify when the goal will be achieved. Useful goals do not simply roll on into a vague future; they must be achieved 'by...'.

A discussion about 'by when?' can often lead to a modification in the details of a goal. For example, a plan for helping a child in her language development might seem too ambitious once you ask, 'When is she likely to have made this kind of progress?' You may need to break your initial plan into finer steps. Often, it will be more appropriate to set a date to review progress towards a goal, rather than imply that it should be fully achieved by the given date.

Involvement

The individual who is responsible for a goal has to feel personally involved and motivated. If you are a senior worker, you might help other staff to identify appropriate goals for their practice. Alternatively your responsibilities might include close work with individual parents, perhaps on handling their children's behaviour. Part of your discussion will be to ensure that the other person feels involved and will commit personally to this goal – rather than taking the line of 'All right, if you say so.'

You are more likely to encourage involvement if you explore both the concerns of the other person and the benefits of achieving this realistic goal.

EXAMPLES

Look at the following attempts to set goals in an early years centre. Using the guidelines for useful goals, consider what questions you would ask and the issues you would explore to reach more useful goals.

- In supervision, Marcella suggests her personal goal is to attend some external training courses this year. She has been very resistant to any further training so far.
- Peter accepts that his report-writing needs to be improved. He promises that he will try to make the reports a bit better organised and get them in on time more often, as well as improve his spelling.

- Laura suggests at a staff meeting that the centre should aim to be more involved in the local community and take a higher profile in local early years campaigns.
- Nazish is concerned about four-year-old Martin's eating. Martin has a very narrow range of foods that he is prepared to try and takes a considerable amount of time over every meal. Nazish aims to introduce one new food to Martin each week and within a month to have encouraged him to finish his meal at the same time as the other children.

Supporting teamwork
Building trust

Continuing trust is crucial for good working relationships. It is the key to building and maintaining an effective early years team. Your trust in your colleagues, and theirs in you, grows from direct experience of how people behave in their work. Trust is created especially from experience that colleagues are:

- *reliable* – that people follow through on their work commitments. They do what they said they would do, in the way and to the time scale that was agreed. If they cannot complete a task they have started, they will say so;
- *consistent* – that they can be depended upon to work to a good standard every day, or every session. The quality of their work does not vary with their mood, with personal problems outside work or whether or not they have warmed to a child or parent;
- *honest* – that they will express openly what they feel and act in the best interests of colleagues.

Asking that workers should be reliable is not the same as requiring that they are perfect. You will feel more able to trust colleagues who are confident to ask questions if they are confused, or who ask for help before they are in a serious muddle. In order for trust to develop, individual workers need to feel that their colleagues, including the centre manager, will react positively to requests for assistance or information. Workers who feel dismissed or belittled will decide that any claims of 'we're a team here' are empty talk.

Teams and their leaders need to build up trust; it grows with honesty and positive experiences of each other. Admitting that there is a lack of trust in your team is *not* the same as accusing colleagues of deceit or dishonesty. A low level of trust in practice will usually mean that workers are uncertain; they lack confidence in each other. Past experience may make team members uneasy. As a result, they are more likely to check up on colleagues with, 'Have you finished that report on Siobhan?' or 'You haven't forgotten we're being inspected next week?'

Being chased in this way can feel like nagging. You may need to discuss the experience and the feelings with the other person. Sometimes more general issues should be aired in a team meeting.

3.2 Organising a team

Two key objectives in organising a group of early years workers are to ensure:

- continuity of the curriculum for children, so that they have opportunities to learn steadily. The organisation of workers (and the plans; see section 1.5) provide links between what is offered from day to day;
- constancy of workers' presence and behaviour with children. Organisation of workers between different groups or by shifts should support the development of close and stable relationships between staff and children. Professional behaviour for early years workers requires involvement – *not* a sense of detachment from babies and children. Appropriately affectionate and caring relationships are crucial for children's well-being.

If the scope of your centre also includes close work with parents, then continuity and constancy are equally important in this aspect of your job.

Roles and responsibilities

In your centre there will be a long list of tasks that have to be completed. Some will be regular daily, or weekly responsibilities, whilst some responsibilities arise as you organise a special event or face changes. Broadly, workers' roles will be made clear by their job description. However, there will always be further detail which reflects the inevitable changes in daily work.

Being clear about roles

Fixed roles?
Centres vary in the extent to which they have relatively fixed roles for individuals. The apparent advantage of a fixed pattern is that there is little uncertainty, since the same worker takes on the same set of tasks all the time.

Forward planning determines who will take the responsibility for which activity

Workers are familiar with what they are doing so there is less need for instruction. However, the attractions of a fixed pattern are also the source of its disadvantages. Fixed responsibilities remove uncertainty; unfortunately they also remove variety and the opportunity for workers to extend their skills. In short, the work can become boring and workers who have lost interest will not be stimulating companions for babies and children.

Specific responsibilities
Not all tasks within a centre should be rotated around the staff group. Some may have to be the responsibility of a more senior worker. Continuity may require that no more than one or two workers take responsibility for developments such as a group run for parents. Some roles may become confusing if shared by several people, for example, having more than one worker to deal with formal complaints from parents.

Using a rota

The centre manager should ensure that all workers understand their role and what is expected of them, both in terms of their regular responsibilities and those that rotate around the staff group. (See also 'delegation' on page 32.)

The most practical way to plan ahead for a centre is to draw up a rota. This will typically be for several weeks ahead and includes all the tasks that will pass around workers, including any volunteers. The rota needs to be displayed where all workers can easily consult it. In drawing up a rota you have to allow for all the key tasks that need to be completed within the centre but other considerations will also influence your plans. For instance:

● Look for opportunities for individual workers to use special skills or talents, such as knowledge of songs in different languages or a flair for story-telling.
● A rota can be used to support workers in extending their skills and building confidence. A less confident worker may need support initially and the rota can pair her or him with a more experienced worker.
● In centres with male and female workers, the rota can ensure that children are given a non-stereotyped image of how women and men can work.

Creative use of the rota can bring variety and interest for workers and children alike. However, a rota should never result in unpredictable changes of staff that are likely to disrupt children.

The key worker system

Babies and children can only form stable and affectionate relationships if they are able to relate to a small number of familiar adults. Good practice is to have a key worker (or primary worker) system in which individual members of staff take a specific responsibility for a group of children.

The key worker completes the children's records and individual plans for learning and keeps close contact with children's parents. The relationship is not exclusive – certainly not a case of 'my children' as opposed to 'your children'. Key workers relate to other children, to colleagues and to parents. The advantage is that children, parents (and where appropriate other professionals) are able to develop a relationship with a worker who is closely involved and knowledgeable about a small number of children or babies.

Children's long-term emotional attachments are with their parents, or in some families with others in a parental role. The role of key worker can be difficult when parents feel uneasy about their child's strong attachment to another adult. Uncomfortable situations can also arise if workers and parents disagree over a child's development or welfare. Whilst these potential drawbacks to the key worker system are insufficient reason to opt for detached relationships, key workers may need the support of more senior colleagues when difficulties arise.

Diversity in the team
The multi-disciplinary team

Staff members may not share the same qualifications. A multi-disciplinary team is more usual in family centres or combined care/education settings but may develop in other early years centres. Staff with different professional backgrounds can bring a fresh perspective but this diversity needs to be co-ordinated effectively. If you are a manager, then set the pattern.

- Show actively that you value workers' different skills, whether or not these emerge from the particular professional qualification.
- Involve all staff members in planning and decision-making. Avoid situations in which staff with a particular qualification are allowed to dominate meetings. The situation is different if their expertise is particularly relevant to the issue under discussion.
- You may be part of a hierarchy about which you have little choice. For instance, social services or the local education authority may insist that more senior workers have a particular qualification. Or there may be different conditions of service for workers depending on their qualifications. There is no point in hitting your head against a brick wall that you cannot dismantle. Accept what you cannot change and focus on making the situation as positive as possible.

Other sources of diversity

All centres will have the benefits of some variety within the staff group. The full resources of a team might include individuals who have:

- talents and interests in craft activities or music;
- sound knowledge of different cultures or religions;
- ability in more than one spoken language or experience in sign language;
- insight from personal experience, for instance, of being a parent or of the impact of continuing health conditions on families;
- specific skills, for instance, in counselling or physiotherapy.

A manager should ensure that no potential skills of any worker are overlooked. However, the existing pattern of skills should not be seen as fixed. A centre should provide workers with the opportunity to extend their existing skills. However, workers with specialisms should not be trapped into a narrow role.

ACTIVITY

All staff groups include some diversity in background, skills and interests which can be an asset to the team. Conduct a 'skills and experience audit' of your own team.

- Think as broadly as possible about variety within the group and avoid being misled by outward similarities. You could explore this issue in a team meeting or through individual conversations.

- Ask workers to describe their particular talents, interests and areas of knowledge. Stress, if need be, that you are not requiring immense expertise.

Expertise needs to be shared – but clearly

TO THINK ABOUT

Please consider the following examples of using the special knowledge or experience of individual workers.

- Sarah's husband works for a Japanese firm and Sarah has joined him on two trips to the Far East. Several Japanese families are living in company houses and have sent their children to the playgroup. The playgroup leader has asked Sarah to be key worker for the children.
- In the after-school club, Derek is the only worker who has children of his own. His younger colleagues prefer him to deal with the parents when a child's behaviour has been so disruptive that something needs to be said.
- Sian is bilingual in Welsh and English and has a special interest in story-telling. She takes a group of children for story-telling and songs once a week in her own playgroup and visits two others in the neighbourhood.
- Ayesha's family came originally from the Caribbean. She is the only black member of staff in the private nursery where she works and has become aware that the manager expects her to deal with all the black parents.
- Piya is the only worker in his community nursery who has experience of working with children with severe hearing loss. The manager asks Piya if he will teach two other workers some basic signs and draw up a play programme for a profoundly deaf child who is about to join the nursery.
- Nina spent several years of her childhood in a residential home before being adopted. A colleague wants her to become joint leader of the centre's group for parents, many of whom had a disrupted childhood.
- Greg is a talented woodworker and coaches the local under-11s football team. The leader of his after-school club asks Greg to take responsibility for both of these activities during the summer holiday programme.

1 To what extent do you feel the way of organising is appropriate?
2 If the use of the worker is inappropriate, how would you explain your reservations to the manager of this centre?
3 What might be a more suitable use of this worker's talents?

Male workers

In the early years field, female workers considerably outnumber males. Many centres have totally female staff groups. One explanation is that work with babies and young children is still viewed predominantly as women's work. However, male workers are not always made welcome, even in centres who would like to believe they take gender issues seriously. Men who wish to enter early years child care and education often have to face surprise from others at their choice of career. With the increased awareness of child abuse, they may also face suspicion – from both staff and parents.

There are two, equally important issues within early years work which tend to lead a team or a management committee to contradictory conclusions:

- *Equal opportunities on gender*: A key principle underlying good practice is that early years workers should challenge stereotypes about rigid roles for girls and boys, men and women. If a team includes male workers this offers very positive opportunities to show that men are competent and caring with babies and children. A male worker can provide a positive male role model for all the children, but especially for those whose family situation offers limited contact with men.
- *Child protection*: The majority of convicted child abusers are men. The concern is that allowing men to work with young children, who necessarily need close physical care and contact, could place children at risk. Some centres employ male workers but ban them from giving any personal care to children.

The decision reached by following either principle has both advantages and potential drawbacks for children and for a centre.

Making a policy decision

The position of male workers in an early years team has to be discussed and resolved openly. Such a discussion should not be postponed until a male worker is about to join the team. Every worker should know the policy on this issue and be able to explain the reasons to parents, new staff and volunteers.

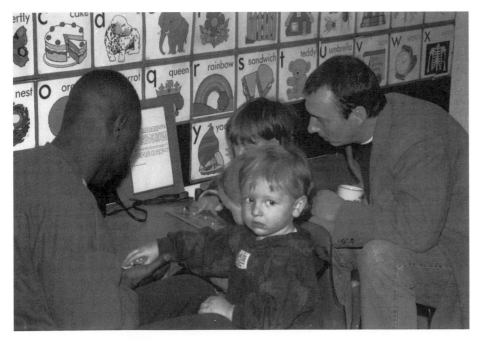

Parents will also bring skills and ideas to enrich the team

If the policy is to restrict the role of male workers, then be ready to explain the reasons to observant children who ask why a male worker cannot change the baby or take a child to the bathroom. Perhaps your centre policy is to have male and female workers covering the same child-care role. Then you may need to be ready for conversations with parents who are worried about men in child care. Alternatively, some parents may have strong beliefs, rooted in their culture or religion, against male involvement in 'women's work'.

On balance, we would recommend that it is better practice to involve men fully in child care than to exclude them. Some women abuse children, so focusing on men as the only source of risk can create a false sense of security. It is also unjust and insulting to the vast majority of men who do not abuse. If male workers' roles are restricted, then children are left with the conviction that only women (workers or mothers) should be doing particular tasks with children.

All centres need to have thorough checks on incoming staff – whether paid or voluntary. The best protection is then to:

- help children learn about appropriate and inappropriate touching and understand personal privacy;
- ensure that all workers are sensitive to children's wishes;
- establish for all staff physical care routines that protect children;
- ensure that any concerns expressed by children are taken seriously.

Reading on . . .

★ Hyder, Tina and Kenway, Penny 1995: *An Equal Future: A guide to anti-sexist practice in the early years* (National Early Years Network).

★ Ruxton, Sandy 1992: '*What's he doing at the Family Centre?' The dilemmas of men who care for children* (Report for National Children's Home – NCH).

★ There is also a relevant section in Whalley, Margy 1994: *Learning to be Strong: Setting up a neighbourhood service for under-fives and their families* (Hodder and Stoughton).

3.3 Communication within the team

TO THINK ABOUT

A centre will be overloaded if all information is passed on to everyone.

- You notice that the outside climbing frame has a loose bolt.
- You plan to take four children to the library.
- A speech therapist has given the centre a set of suggestions for supporting children whose language development is delayed.
- A father phones to say that his child is in hospital with suspected meningitis.
- You notice head lice in the hair of one child.
- A child who has reacted to minor frustrations with fierce tantrums seems to be responding well to the approach of his key worker.
- A mother confides to you that she had a miscarriage last week.
- A parent tells you that a boy, who lives next door to her, is absent from the centre because 'his uncle has been knocking him about again.'

1 In what way should the kinds of information listed above be communicated within the centre?
2 What should be passed on to parents or to professionals outside the centre?

Honest expression of views

Positive communications will depend on an assertive approach from individuals within the team. Assertion is often confused with aggressiveness, so it is important to distinguish between this and a submissive approach.

Assertion – 'We first'
If you behave in an assertive way then you are:

- standing up for your own rights, but in such a way that you do not dismiss or ignore the rights of other people;
- expressing your wants, opinions, feelings and beliefs in a direct and honest way and allowing space for the ideas and experience contributed by others.

The positive consequences of assertion are that members of a team are open with each other. Concerns and ideas are expressed honestly, without long delays and with an awareness of the possible effects on others.

Submissive behaviour – 'You first'
People who behave in a submissive way (sometimes called 'passive' or 'non-assertive') aim to avoid conflict and to please others. They may express their opinions apologetically or offer a contribution in a self-effacing style that almost invites dismissal. They act as if they believe that other people's rights are more important than theirs and their contribution is less valuable.

If you take a submissive approach, you may feel you are being helpful within the team, perhaps by saying, 'I don't mind' or 'If it's all right with you'. Yet the result is a lack of honesty about feelings and denying the team your contribution. Despite not speaking up, you may still feel resentment that 'I had a good idea but nobody asked me'. This annoyance may simmer under the surface and emerge later, to disrupt colleagues who are genuinely perplexed by your feelings.

Good communication will mean messages are passed on

Aggression – 'Me first'

When people take an aggressive approach (verbally or physically), they are motivated by the desire to win regardless of whether this is at the expense of others. People who behave aggressively are standing up for their own rights but are behaving in such a way that they violate the rights of others, regarding them as less important.

If you take an aggressive approach, this may lead you to feel powerful. You may believe forcefulness and bluntness are assets but disrespect can rebound on others. For instance, aggression towards parents or other professionals can create bad feeling that undermines the work of colleagues and may provoke aggression in return.

TO THINK ABOUT

Look at the comments that follow and decide which of them show an assertive approach, which are submissive and which are aggressive. Discuss your ideas with colleagues. (Answers on page 76.)

a) 'The problem with you is that you always think you're right. Just because you've worked in a school, you think you can lord it over the rest of us.'

b) 'I expect this isn't really important. Probably it's because I'm not a physiotherapist. But isn't Dolan's therapy actually making her worse?'

c) 'I'm concerned. I think the parents who help us in the club aren't getting enough explanation before they start, so they're making mistakes that could be avoided.'

d) 'Maybe I've got the wrong impression about this trip. I suppose you know best, but shouldn't we have a few more adults in the group?'

e) Jerry, we've spoken before about your behaviour towards parents. If there is any repetition of what happened this morning, I'll have no choice but to start disciplinary action. I would prefer not to do that.'

f) 'That just won't work with this kind of family. If you'd worked with children for twenty years like I have, then you'd understand.'

g) 'Winston, I would really like your contribution to the playgroup's annual report by Friday at the latest. Can you do that?'

h) 'I'm terribly sorry; I know this is short notice, but would you mind very much if I left the keys for you to lock up tonight?'

i) 'I don't know how you can stand there and ask me to listen out for the phone. Can't you see how busy I am?'

j) 'I would prefer not to change shifts with Sandy. I'm taking my daughter to an orthodontic appointment that afternoon. I don't want to cancel it because it'll be months before they give me another date.'

k) 'I appreciate that you're very busy, Saira, but completing the children's records is part of your job.'

1 What are the possible consequences of the non-assertive comments?
2 In what way could you re-phrase the aggressive or submissive comments to make them assertive?

Reading on . . .

★ Back, Ken and Kate 1991: *Assertiveness at Work – A practical guide to handling awkward situations* (McGraw-Hill).

★ Dickson, Anne 1988: *A Woman in Your Own Right: Assertiveness and you* (Quartet).

Dealing with conflict in the team

Workers who trust each other and have established a pattern of positive communication will not be unnerved by disagreements. A confident manager brings differences of opinion into the open and guides constructive discussion. If your centre has a supportive atmosphere then:

- important issues will be raised in a timely way. Doubts will be aired and can then be resolved;
- information will be shared swiftly and can then be evaluated;
- individual workers are likely to feel more committed to the work because their concerns and different views are valued and considered in decision-making;
- decisions are likely to be of better quality because the alternatives have been covered and assumptions have been checked.

Too little conflict

Many people would rather have less disruption than more, but an absence of disagreement in a team is not necessarily a good sign.

- If all workers are utterly in tune, there is the risk of becoming complacent. You become less clear about explaining your reasons in the work, since you have lost sight of the fact that there are other possibilities.
- Some teams have no obvious disagreements but conflicting views are not voiced. Perhaps disagreement is not permitted by a forceful manager but problems will still rumble below the surface. Irritated workers will wait for the manager to fail, or undermine the centre's work by their actions or inaction. Disagreements do not go away unless they are resolved openly.
- Another possibility is that a non-assertive manager avoids even the mildest dissension. Some staff may also prefer to side-step what they view as unpleasantness. Then assumptions go unchecked and information or

Find constructive ways of expressing your opinions!

concerns will not be raised, for fear of rocking the boat. In the worst case, children might be put at risk.

Too much conflict

It is equally possible to have too many disagreements within a team, or to have a divergence of opinion that is badly handled by senior workers. Some teams develop an argumentative style in which conflict is relished for its own sake. The high risk of this situation is that:

- ideas fail to be discussed because winning (or not losing) an argument has become more important than identifying what will help children and parents. Elements of a good idea are lost because it has to be 'all or nothing';
- staff groups can become badly fragmented as workers are forced to take sides and teamwork is lost. Those who do not relish the conflict can experience serious stress;
- the morale of the team plummets as personal interests dominate and everyone loses sight of the objectives of the centre. Children will suffer as a result.

Handling disagreements positively

A team in which individuals respect one another can deal with arguments, so long as a constructive pattern is set by the manager and senior workers.

- A manager should encourage staff in good communication, especially to:
  – listen as well as express their own perspective;
  – be specific about 'what' and 'when';
  – avoid sweeping statements such as 'you always interrupt' or 'you never put the files away'.
- Everyone should try hard not to see disagreement as a personal affront.
- Individuals need to let incidents go and not hark back once the issues are resolved.

Teams benefit from an assertive approach (see also page 64) in which feelings and views are expressed honestly, yet with consideration for others. An assertive statement about a problem situation will have some, or all of the following elements:

- A brief description of the event or the issue – for example, 'When you presented the special needs report to the management committee...'.
- Your feelings, expressed honestly – 'I felt angry...'.
- A brief explanation – 'because you didn't say that I wrote half of it...'.
- What you would rather have happen – 'I would prefer that you either write my name on the report with yours or tell the committee how much work I put in'. (Do not give more than one option, unless you are genuinely happy with either.)

A time and a place

Everyone has a responsibility to resolve conflicts in the team – not just senior workers – so that a poor atmosphere does not sour the work with children and families. It is equally important that disagreements between workers are not expressed in front of the children or parents. A manager should explain firmly that this is unacceptable behaviour. As hard as it may feel to an aggrieved worker, any irritation must be handled with the person concerned and not vented on someone else – child or adult.

Persistent problems between individuals

Some disagreements fail to be resolved through informal discussion and require a more organised approach. The individuals involved then have to:

- find a time to talk – conflict, rather than minor disagreements, will not be resolved in a snatched couple of moments;
- find a place for an uninterrupted conversation;
- talk through the issues; and finally
- reach an agreement that will resolve the conflict.

Productive talking

The best way to manage differences between people is to talk face-to-face about the issues on which you differ and to talk without interruption for as long as necessary to reach a breakthrough.

You may be involved in this kind of conversation because you disagree with a colleague, or a parent, and are motivated to do something about the impasse. Alternatively, as a third party, you may be bringing together two people who will not themselves resolve an entrenched conflict.

Be positive and optimistic
- Open the conversation by expressing your appreciation that the other person is willing to talk and be optimistic that the conversation will help.
- *Briefly* describe the issue as you see it and then invite the other person to put their view. (Alternatively you might invite each of the people in dispute to say how they see the situation.)

Open communication
- Listen to what the other person is saying. (Or encourage two people in dispute to take turns in listening.)
- Avoid interrupting the other person unless you need to summarise in order to understand. (As a third party, you may need to intervene if one person is dominating the talk time.)
- Summarise what you have heard to check that you understand. There is no point in offering advice or suggestions until you have grasped the perspective of the other person. (Encourage two other people in dispute to summarise.)
- If necessary, redirect the other person back to the issue if he or she appears to be wandering from the main point.
- Acknowledge that the situation may feel difficult but express optimism that 'I feel sure we can find some way through'.
- Acknowledge the feelings of the other person and, if appropriate, express your own feelings, but not as a way to blame the other person. (See also page 110 on dealing with angry parents, since the points made are equally applicable when workers are angry.)
- Be clear about what you need or want to say. The conversation should be two-way, yet you may have to express professional concerns about which you have limited choice. Such issues might arise in a conversation with a parent or with colleagues.

Willingness to negotiate
Your aim in the conversation is to encourage a collaboration of us-against-the problem – in contrast to a power battle of me-against-you. You need to take two related approaches:

- *Separate the person from the problem* – work hard not to be drawn into argument about personal foibles or who is to blame for what. Focus on what has happened, the issues that have arisen and what could be done.
- *Focus on interests and not positions* – some conflicts are fuelled by one or both people's insistence on their exact view winning the argument. An emphasis on shared concerns (for a child) and similar interests (in preventing this mistake in the future) can create a more positive discussion.

Acknowledge any conciliatory gestures from the other person. Perhaps your colleague admits, 'I didn't realise the auditor was so strict. Maybe I overreacted when you kept asking me about the petty cash receipts'. You should reply with something like, 'Well, I'm glad I've had the chance to explain it properly to you'. The conversation will go sour if you try to score points with, 'I should think you did overreact! Are you going to say "Sorry" now?' Even if someone is more open to your view, do not assume the conflict is over, continue with the conversation to resolve the issue fully.

A constructive agreement has to be reached which will stand a good chance of avoiding future conflict on this issue. A workable agreement *feels* balanced. For example, 'I agree not to check up on the petty cash receipts until the last Tuesday of each month and you agree to have all the paperwork organised for that date'. Such deals have to be very clear, for the obligations of both sides: what is each person committing to do, by when, to what standard (if appropriate) and with what help?

Consider writing down the agreement. Sometimes you may judge that verbal commitment is sufficient. However, a written record would be appropriate for any conflicts over standards in the centre or very heated disagreements.

When conflict cannot be resolved

You will not manage to resolve conflict if:

- you do not give the conversation enough time;
- you do not apply the approach whole-heartedly, for instance, you are more interested in winning than finding a genuine compromise. Or if the other person refuses to make any compromise;
- there is a genuine and unresolvable difference of interests;
- the other person is committed to an aggressive approach, perhaps physically;
- the other person has a distorted sense of reality, for instance, through alcohol or drug abuse. Personal safety becomes an issue with this and the previous point.

If you judge that further conversation with a parent or worker will not make a difference, you will close the discussion with a summary of the situation as it remains. Perhaps you will explain how a parent can take her issue forward as a formal complaint (see page 113). Or you may state the consequences if a worker continues with the behaviour that has led to the current discussion. You should write down a summary of what has been said and explain this to the other person.

Reading on . . .

★ Dana, Daniel 1990: *Talk it Out: 4 steps to managing people problems in your organisation* (Kogan Page).

Answers to 'THINK ABOUT' box on page 65

- Assertive comments: c, e, g, j, k
- Submissive comments: b, d, h
- Aggressive comments: a, f, i

3.4 Planning and running meetings

Different kinds of meetings

Much important communication in early years centres will take place informally as people meet in parts of the centre or talk to each other while working. Yet a proportion of communication will take place in more formal meetings. All centres should have meetings, although they will not all experience every type of meeting.

Staff meetings

All centres should have regular full staff meetings, since this is the only way to ensure that important information is communicated to everyone. These provide opportunities for concerns to be raised, problems resolved and decisions made. Effective team meetings can have a positive impact on a sense of working together and feeling valued.

Room meetings

In centres with several group rooms, there may be meetings between a senior worker and the two or three room staff. Such meetings are an opportunity to discuss the progress of individual children and the approach to parents. In a similar way, a key worker might meet with a senior worker to discuss the children and families for which the key worker is primarily responsible. (See page 59 for key worker system.)

Centre meetings

Open meetings may be held specifically for parents in order to provide an exchange of views or for specific discussions, for instance, following an inspection report on the centre. If you work in a school, there may be regular meetings called by the Parent–Teacher Association or Friends of the school.

Reviews

Local authority children's and family centres will have meetings to review the place offered to a child and family. Parents should always be invited to these meetings. It is also likely that the family's health visitor and their social worker, if they have one, will be invited to attend.

Case conferences

Any early years worker could be involved in a case conference, but you are more likely to be involved if you work in a local authority children's or family centre working with a number of families who are under stress. A range of other professionals will be invited to a case conference, as well as parents.

Committee meetings

If your centre is run by a management committee, then there will be regular meetings between the committee members and the centre manager. Sometimes, other members of staff may be asked to attend so that they can give a specific report on some part of the centre's work. If you work in a playgroup, then your centre may be set up with a steering group, a constitution and the obligation to have a given number of meetings every year, including an Annual General Meeting. (See also section 2.4.)

Effective meetings

TO THINK ABOUT

Before you read this section, consider two meetings that you have attended within the last month. Pick one meeting that you feel was well run and another that, in your experience, was ineffective in one or more ways.

● Note down exactly what happened in the first meeting that demonstrated it was time well spent.
● Then describe the badly-run meeting. What went wrong and how? What would be the main changes to achieve an improvement in the future?

Now read on.

Clear aims for the meeting

In a well-prepared and well-run meeting everyone will know the answer to the key questions of 'Why are we meeting?' and 'What am I contributing?'

In a staff meeting you may want to achieve several objectives:

● to review the events of last week and to plan for next week;
● to share information and expertise within the team;
● to take some decisions affecting the centre;
● to gather suggestions or ideas for solving a problem.

It can be difficult to discuss broader issues of good practice and the weekly business of a centre within the same meeting. A manager may decide to have a separate meeting in order to focus on, for instance, a detailed review of the centre's practice in developmental records for children.

Other kinds of meetings, especially those involving centre workers, parents and other early years professionals, can become confused unless there has been clear communication of the aims of the meeting.

Inappropriate issues for a meeting

A necessary condition for an effective meeting is that a meeting is the best way to do this piece of work.

Formal meetings are not the place for general conversation and catching up with colleagues. Meetings can recognise the achievements of staff and give a vote of thanks. They should not be a forum for detailed individual feedback, whether positive or negative; this should be made within supervision (see section 4.2). Issues that are relevant only to a couple of individuals should be resolved outside the larger meeting.

Agendas

Well-run meetings have an agenda that is drawn up and circulated to everyone attending, before the meeting takes place. Agendas should give start and finish times and a complete list of items to be covered. Sometimes it makes sense to give an approximate length of time for each item. Certainly, the person who draws up the agenda needs to be realistic about how much can be covered in the time available. Management committee meetings will have a more formal agenda than, for instance, a team meeting (see the examples box on page 72).

Agendas can only guide meetings if they are followed. Part of the role of the chair in any meeting is to keep everyone focused on the agreed agenda.

✠ **EXAMPLES**

As the leader of St Mark's Playgroup, Sally draws up the agenda for their bi-monthly team meeting. She shows a draft agenda to everyone three days before the meeting and finalises the items on the day before.

St Mark's team meeting, Monday 8th January, 4.00 to 5.00 pm.

1 Issues with the children and families:
   - Malaika – observations on Sean's behaviour in the playgroup. Decisions about a consistent approach to his physical aggression.
   - Anne – update on the conversation group with the four-year-olds.
   - Celebrating Chinese New Year and how we present this to parents.

2 Reports:
   - Philip's plans for his GNVQ child development study.
   - Sally's meeting with the Church council over playgroup security measures.

3 Ideas and initial plans for the summer fete.

Sally also attends meetings of the playgroup management committee, at which the agenda is drawn up by the committee secretary and circulated two weeks before the meeting.

St Mark's management committee, 18 March, 7.00 to 8.30 pm.

1 Welcome and attendance
2 Apologies for absence
3 Minutes of the last meeting
(Minutes are circulated in advance and signed by the committee chair after any necessary amendments.)
4 Matters arising from the minutes
(This includes progress reports on any work that members agreed to undertake.)
5 Correspondence
(Plus discussion of any necessary action arising.)
6 Financial report
(From the treasurer. This would be the annual accounts during the AGM.)
7 Reports
(Sally has been asked to report on the playgroup's approach to non-Christian festivals, since two parents who attend St Mark's church have complained to the management committee about the Chinese New Year celebrations.)
8 Special items to be discussed
(Items not covered under other agenda items.)
9 Date of next meeting
10 Any other business
(The chair is firm in closing down potentially lengthy discussions and placing them as reports or special items on the next agenda.)

General preparation

Preparation for a meeting will also involve practical issues of organisation:

- deciding on or actually booking a room for the meeting;
- ensuring there are enough chairs and any necessary equipment such as a flip-chart;
- organising simple refreshments;
- making arrangements for who will answer the telephone or switching on the answerphone.

During the meeting

Chairing

This role may be taken by the same person each meeting, for instance the leader of the management committee. The centre manager might always chair team meetings, but there are advantages in rotating this task. All staff can then learn first hand the skills of keeping a team focused and dealing with conflicting views or silences.

Long meetings become unproductive

The main tasks of chairing are to:

- keep the meeting timely, making sure that later items are not rushed because earlier ones have been allowed too much time;
- follow the agenda. This task includes keeping everyone informed of the transition from one agenda item to another and ensuring that the discussion does not ramble. It can help if the chair summarises the main points covered on one item, and actions resulting, before moving on to the next. A summary can be especially helpful to the meeting if a discussion has been lengthy or has involved disagreement;
- encourage everyone to participate in the meeting. The chair may have to invite contributions from quieter people and courteously quieten the more vocal individuals;
- make sure that key decisions and issues are recorded. The chair could take notes in a team meeting but this task should be delegated to someone else in a more formal meeting. In an open discussion of ideas, the best form of noting can be to write on a flip-chart, so that everyone can see. The points have to be copied up later;
- ease the entry and departure of anyone who attends only part of a meeting. In reviews and case conferences it would not be appropriate for parents, for instance, to sit through the entire meeting. The chair should courteously introduce any visitor to the meeting and ensure that the relevant issues are discussed while that person is present;
- remain objective. If you are chairing a meeting, you should not allow your own perspective to determine how you invite other contributions or how you sum up a discussion. If you have a specific contribution to make to a meeting, such as a report, then it is better to hand over the chairing role to another person while you make your presentation.

Encouraging equal participation

Chairing a very quiet meeting, in which there are few contributions, can be as hard as controlling an outspoken group. You may, of course, chair a mixed meeting with both highly vocal and very quiet people.

Ground rules should ideally be agreed at the beginning of a meeting. Such rules determine how people will interact, whereas the agenda focuses on the content of the meeting.

Possible ground rules for very lively groups:

- 'Only one person talks at a time.' The chair must enforce and follow this rule.
- 'Say three good things' is a tactic that asks everyone to focus on the benefits of someone else's contribution before taking the floor with their own. (This tactic can be very useful for groups who often say 'Yes, but...'.)
- Adopt a ground rule for part, if not all of the meeting, that everyone must accurately summarise what the previous person has said before starting their own contribution. This rule helps people to listen to others.

Suggestions for very quiet groups:

- Early in the meeting organise a 'round robin' in which everyone says something on the topic in turn, however briefly.
- Invite suggestions in written form to be given to the chair before the meeting.
- The chair asks quieter members to comment – before that person has been silent for too long. The chair can tell the individual before the meeting that his or her contribution will be invited on a specific topic.

Taking minutes

There should be a written record of any meeting. This record, usually called 'the minutes', should be made available to everyone who attended and any absentees. A room meeting or discussion between a key worker and senior in a centre will also benefit from some notes of what was decided.

To be useful and reliable, minutes must be taken during the meeting and *not* afterwards from memory. They should include:

- where and when the meeting took place and who attended, including absentees;
- ideas that were expressed but are not earmarked for action as yet;
- concerns or issues that were not resolved but must not be forgotten;
- information that should be noted;
- decisions that were taken;
- actions that individuals have agreed to undertake. Minutes should include a clear record of what is to be done, by whom and by when.

In a formal meeting, such as a management committee meeting, completed minutes would be typed up afterwards. In a team meeting, a clear handwritten set of minutes can work well. You can use underlining or asterisks to highlight key points. The chair would also ask workers to make a personal note of what they have agreed to do.

The notes of any meeting should always be taken with attention to accuracy and detail. This can be especially important when a case conference has been called on a child and family. When there is concern over child protection, case conference notes might later have to be produced in court (under the Children Act 1989).

ACTIVITY

Please try some of the suggestions given here during a meeting that you chair.

1   How well did these tactics work?
2   What other suggestions would you add to the list that you have found to work?

TO THINK ABOUT

You should be ready to give reasons for taking minutes. For example, a parent invited into a review or case conference might be wary of the purpose of written notes. Good practice would be to explain why notes are made and to give parents a copy of the minutes relating to their part of the meeting.

Reporting to a meeting

Meetings can be the best way for a group of people to listen to a report from an individual. Anyone who is going to be asked to give a report should be forewarned so that they can prepare and bring all the relevant information.

If you are asked to report to a meeting, your contribution might just be oral. However, on occasions you could be presenting highlights of a written report or taking the meeting through important information that you present using simple visual aids, such as paper copies of information or a flip-chart.

It is worth preparing for any kind of report to a meeting, even if your contribution will be relatively brief.

- Think about the key points that you wish to make and note them down. This approach will help you remember all your points and to place emphasis where you wish. Plan a logical sequence to your points.
- Sometimes, you may submit a written report to the meeting (see also section 2.3). If you give this out to the meeting, people will immediately

---

 CASE STUDY

In Mount Park Children's Centre, Leela introduced a one page guidance sheet to help her staff to prepare for reviews. Some of the less experienced workers were uneasy about speaking up, especially in front of social workers, and tended to give very uneven reports on children. The guidance sheet covered:

- general information such as a child's name and age and how long they had attended the centre;
- children's pattern of attendance, such as how well they had settled in (if newly arrived) and patterns of non-attendance;
- general physical well-being of children, including current height and weight;
- detailed highlights of children's developmental progress;
- the involvement of any other professionals with the child, for instance, doctor or speech therapist;
- a description of children's relationships – with other children, workers and parents;

- the relationship between centre workers and the child's parents;
- overall conclusions, including any concerns.

The reports are given verbally to the review meeting by the relevant worker and also written up. Leela has worked hard with her team on achieving reports that are honest and informative, yet as positive as possible.

1 Would you add any other broad areas to Leela's list? Are there any other issues on which you would brief workers if there were child protection concerns about an individual child?

2 Do you have any guidance notes in your centre to support workers as they prepare a verbal or written report for a meeting? If yes, then please look at one set of guidance notes with a view to finding any improvements that could be made. If your answer is no, then draft some helpful notes to support a regular report that workers have to make. Show your draft to a colleague for comment.

start to flick through the pages and stop listening to you. An alternative is to prepare a few flip-chart sheets and guide your talk with these. Then hand out the report to everyone when you are finished.

- Avoid reading a report word for word, unless you are so nervous about the presentation that this is really the only way you can manage.
- Decide in advance whether you wish to take questions as you go along or when you have finished. It is much easier to keep to time if you take questions at the end.

Reading on . . .

Most of the general books on management in Appendix 3 have a section on meetings. For brief and practical pointers try:

★   *How to Run a Meeting: Making meetings more productive* and *More Bloody Meetings: The people side of meetings* (booklets from Video Arts Ltd).

4 Developing staff

This chapter covers:

- new workers in a centre;
- support and supervision;
- staff development;
- poor standards and discipline.

4.1 New workers

Recruitment and selection
Advertising and the short-list

You need to follow a consistent process in seeking new staff. The approach to advertising, short-listing and interviewing should ensure that the best potential source of workers is sought. You will have to advertise in publications likely to be read by prospective workers: national newspapers or magazines, local newspapers and internal newsletters in your organisation.

To draft a useful advertisement, you have to think about the job that is vacant and the qualities and experience that you are seeking. Legal restraints mean that a centre or a management committee cannot decide arbitrarily to seek only female workers (against the Sex Discrimination Act 1976) or to employ only certain racial groups (against the Race Relations Act 1976). A centre might sometimes reasonably seek a new worker with specific skills or background. Good practice would be to write a person specification that shows how certain qualities are essential for this post. You could use this brief for reference but would not insert it all into the advertisement.

Principles of equal opportunities should run through staff selection as much as in other aspects of the work. Consider all the applications in the light of the post that you have advertised. Follow up references for all your short-listed candidates.

Interviewing

Successful interviewing starts with your own preparation through the following steps:

- Remind yourself of the qualities and experience that you are seeking in the person who takes this post. During the interviewing process you should compare individual candidates against the job and not against

Job specifications have to be realistic

each other. You want to be confident that your choice is a person suitable for the role and not the best of a mediocre group.

1   Prepare a list of the questions you will ask each applicant. Note any that are specific to individuals. For instance, one candidate has a special area of expertise or another seems to have left the previous job under a cloud – 'What happened?'

2   Decide whether one person will interview all the candidates, perhaps the manager, or whether there will be a panel. Facing a panel can be more daunting for candidates, but is more effective for a management committee than arranging a series of interviews with each committee member. If the interview will be by panel, then you should have discussed the issues together. Plan who will ask which questions; you do not want panel members interrupting each other.

3   Let the applicants know in advance what will be involved in the interviewing process.

4   Organise a schedule to time a succession of events, such as a chance for applicants to look around the centre, a time for the formal interview and for any group discussion or task that is part of the process.

5   Ensure that there will be no interruptions, except in genuine emergencies. Assign another worker to deal with the telephone and any visitors.

6   Make sure that the room for the interviews is laid out – rearranged if necessary – so that it will seat everyone comfortably. The interviewee needs to be able easily to look at the manager or a panel of people.

Interviewing skills

Effective interviews use good communication skills to obtain answers to relevant questions. The result of an interview is that a decision can be made whether or not to offer the job to a candidate. Since the aim of the selection interview is fact-finding, more control remains with the person doing the interviewing than, for example, in helping a parent talk through a problem or supervision sessions with staff.

● *The pattern of the interview*: Typically, selection interviews start by asking candidates about their general qualifications and experience, then move on to this area of work and their most recent posts. The interview then explores why candidates wish to join this centre and their capability for the post. Finally, candidates should be offered the opportunity to ask their own questions.

● *Using questions and summaries*: Follow a pattern of posing a question, listening to the answer and summarising what you have heard. The point of frequent summaries is to check that you have understood what the applicants said and to give them an opportunity to extend or modify their answers.

Usually, you ask open-ended questions early in the interview. Later, you ask focused questions such as, 'In your last job you ran a group for travellers and their children. How did you organise that work?' Or you might request further information on a reply, for example, 'You said it wasn't easy being the only Asian worker in your previous staff group. Could you say some more about that experience?'

Ask a few 'What if..?' questions to explore how this person might approach some common dilemmas in the centre. You might ask:

> 'Suppose a two-year-old in your care had bitten another child. How would you handle the situation?' or
> 'What would you do if a parent was drunk when she came to pick up her child?'

Make sure that you explore any issues that arise from this candidate's previous experience. It is important to ask potentially difficult questions relevant to how this person will fit into your centre. For instance:

> 'You've never worked with children with disabilities. We have several children here with severe learning and physical disabilities. How do you think you would cope?'

● *Listen and note*: Good interviewers do not interrupt applicants unnecessarily. You may need to intervene courteously if someone is continuing with a long answer. The objective is to learn about the other person, so do not talk about yourself and your work unless it is directly relevant, and then keep it brief.

You should make notes of the applicants' replies, otherwise it will be difficult to remember what was said, especially if you are interviewing several people one after another. If you leave a gap between each interview it will be possible to tidy up brief notes in the interval. If you are part of an interview panel, it is better to keep personal notes and to write these before the panel discusses all the different applicants.

Reading on . . .

★ *It's Your Choice: Selection skills for managers* (Video Arts booklet).
★ Wyatt, Wendy 1995: *How to Employ and Manage Staff: A practical handbook for managers and supervisors* (How To Books).

Terms of employment

Formal agreements state mutual expectations of what is and is not required. Contracts and job descriptions are designed to structure the relationship between the centre and workers and to reduce the likelihood of conflict arising from misunderstandings of what is expected.

Contract of employment

Employers are legally obliged to give contracts to employees who work eight or more hours per week and to produce this contract within two months of the start of employment. However, it is good practice to provide a contract for any paid worker, regardless of hours.

The contract gives the conditions of employment, including salary, hours of work, notice and any sickness and maternity rights associated with the job. If you are involved in checking or drawing up a contract, then consult one of the books suggested in 'Reading on' for details of relevant employment legislation.

The contract does not deal with what you require the person to do on a daily basis; this is the function of a job description.

Job description

All workers should have a written job description that covers the details of a worker's responsibilities. For example, a worker in a sessional playgroup might be required to:

- arrive at 8.30 am to set up for the morning session and leave only after tidying up from the afternoon session that finishes at 3.30 pm;
- supervise and play with the children indoors and in the outdoor play area;
- maintain records on children and families as requested by the manager;
- promote equal opportunities through play and relationships with children and parents;
- welcome parents and carers, encourage their involvement in the group and offer advice when requested; and so on....

The job description should be sufficiently specific that workers can see broadly what is expected of them, but a full understanding will only develop through

Special qualities are needed for working with the very young

conversation and explanation. For instance, 'promote equa▮
would have to be discussed with workers to ensure a consistent a▮

It often helps to have a written agreement with any voluntary help▮
you choose not to put the expectations into writing, then definitely have ▮
conversation in which you cover both the volunteer's and your own
expectations.

Reading on . . .

★ Spicer, Robert 1995: *How to Know Your Rights at Work: A practical guide to employment law* (How To Books).
★ Willison, Jenny 1992: *Running Your Own Playgroup or Nursery* (Kogan Page).
★ 1995: *Pre-schools as Employers* (Pre-school Learning Alliance).

Induction

Neither new workers nor volunteers should be left to find out what is expected without guidance from experienced staff. A useful induction process will usually stretch over several months. Induction needs to be well organised, although it does not have to be highly formal and should include the following:

- An initial, unhurried conversation with a senior member of staff to explain to new workers what they are expected to do and in what way.
- Access to written material about the policies of the centre and the encouragement to talk about the issues once the material has been read. Some centres prepare an induction pack for new workers.
- An individual worker to whom the new member of staff can turn for queries about the daily running of the centre. This experienced worker, sometimes called a mentor, may support the new member of staff during the first year.
- Booked supervision sessions with a senior worker soon after starting so that the new worker can discuss any issues.

Volunteers
Some early years centres have a rota of volunteers whose involvement is crucial to the running of the programme for children. The playgroup movement has a strong tradition of involving parents as helpers, although not all playgroups require parents to join a rota. Some playwork facilities for over-fives have an informal relationship with a number of volunteers.

Unpaid voluntary workers are sometimes left out of the induction process. Yet a regular parent-helper (see page 120), or an interested teenager who has volunteered, needs to understand what should be done in the work and how, just as much as paid staff.

...ources of support within an early years team:

- In ... cooperative atmosphere, workers will offer support to each ... support might be offered in the course of the day or in meetings ... ss the work.
- Senior workers are available for informal conversation and consultation.
- Senior workers arrange regular individual supervision for all staff.

Any centre should work in such a way as to encourage all workers and make them feel that they are valued. It is very difficult, probably impossible, for workers to value the children and parents unless they themselves feel supported and appreciated.

Sometimes two people may solve a problem faster than one

Supervision
The benefits

A regular supervision session can provide the following opportunities:

- Workers can raise specific concerns and problems and discuss possible ways forward.
- An acknowledgement of success with children and parents and giving praise when deserved. Supervision works less well if it is allowed to become the time solely to pick up on what has gone wrong.
- Workers can benefit from discussing broader issues in work and reflecting on their own practice. Some issues can also be raised in group meetings.

- A supervisor can help workers to set priorities and to manage their time when facing conflicting demands.
- Supervision is also the appropriate setting in which to explore a worker's personal learning objectives, including attendance on short courses or more sustained programmes of study.

Effective supervision will be very difficult in a centre lacking consistent direction and clear values. Discussion of the work of one individual can only make real sense within the context of the whole centre.

Senior workers are the most likely and appropriate people to offer regular supervision sessions to other members of the team. The issue then arises of who will supervise and coach the centre manager. In social services, or one of the larger children's charities, a line manager may provide supervision. If this is not the case, centre managers should raise the issue with their direct employer or the management committee.

Skills of supervision

The skills needed to supervise well are those of effective communication. As a supervisor you should:

- listen actively to what is said and be aware of body language;
- reflect back what you hear and summarise feelings and content;
- help a worker to become more specific about ideas or concerns and be specific yourself about suggestions or requirements;
- give constructive feedback and be willing to listen to feedback in your turn;
- encourage a worker to consider other ways of looking at a situation or behaving;
- work together to choose the best way forward;
- use subsequent supervision sessions to follow up on what has happened.

You use similar skills if you are offering help to a parent with difficulties but supervision is a different relationship. Part of responsible supervision is to remain alert to the obligations and boundaries of the work situation. Perhaps a worker feels strongly that a certain course of action would be beneficial for a child, but you might have to remind the worker that this kind of decision has to be left with the child's parents.

Within the supervision relationship, you might offer some help with a worker's personal problems, particularly if such problems were adversely affecting work with children and families. You might, however, have to limit the time made available for very complex personal problems and suggest that the worker arranges for counselling elsewhere.

Reading on . . .

For applications of counselling skills with staff:
★ Hayes, John 1996: *Developing the Manager as a Helper* (Routledge).
★ Humphries, John 1995: *How to Counsel People at Work* (How To Books).
★ Redman, Warren 1995: *Counselling Your Staff* (Kogan Page).

For a more general discussion of counselling:
★ Egan, Gerard 1995: *The Skilled Helper* (Brooks Cole).
★ Murgatroyd, Stephen 1985: *Counselling and Helping* (The British Psychological Society and Methuen).

CASE STUDIES

 1 Salmon Lane Private Nursery

During a rushed supervision session, Teja, a relatively inexperienced worker, was told by Debbie, 'You could really be more active with the children at lunch-time'. Teja turned the comment over in her mind, wondering what exactly Debbie meant, and decided she was being criticised for allowing children to leave food on their plates. Despite the fact that she wished to avoid what felt like nagging over lunch-time, Teja decided to press the children more to finish their meals. In fact, Debbie was not much concerned about empty plates and actually meant that Teja could make meals with the children a more social time by talking with them.

1   What should Teja have done to avoid the misunderstanding?
2   What lessons are there for Debbie?

 2 Walton Green Family Centre

Sergio and Jill jointly run a group room in the family centre. In a room meeting with Maryam (the manager) Sergio was trying to explain to Jill why he feels she 'pushes in' on him when hc is talking with the mothers. Maryam asked, 'Can you give Jill an instance of what you mean?'.

Sergio replied, 'I was talking with Anna's mother last Friday. She was tearful but she seemed comfortable with me. Jill, you came from across the room and interrupted what I was saying. You even stood half in front of me so it was very difficult for me to keep talking with Dawn'.

1   Consider a time when someone on your team needed to become more specific about a concern or irritation. How did you, or anyone else, help them to offer a real example in a constructive way?
2   How might Maryam have taken the session forward if Sergio had been unable to produce any examples to support his general feeling?

 3 Gables Community Nursery

In supervision with Paranjit, Keith discussed his concerns about her record-keeping, and went carefully through the importance of writing up promptly. He also mentioned the two recent incidents when Paranjit left children's files out on a table, instead of replacing them promptly in the filing cabinet. But Keith also made time to say how he had noticed the changes in the children who attended Paranjit's special play sessions – especially Nancy, whose concentration had definitely improved.

1   Describe three recent experiences with colleagues when you worked to communicate a balance of positives as well as negatives.

Be ready to affirm good practice

Planning future learning

Some workers have many ideas for planning their professional development, whereas others are vague on how best to move forward. Supervision sessions are suitable occasions to review needs of individual workers, drawing on the skills of helping and planning. As a supervisor, you should follow these steps:

Step one – Understanding how workers see their future learning
Encourage the worker to express what she would like or thinks she needs to learn. Your skills of listening, of reflecting back and summarising, will help you to understand the worker's perspective. You encourage her to give examples and to be more specific where she is rather vague. You ask workers what they want in their professional development.

Step two – Other perspectives including realistic possibilities within the centre
It is unlikely that a supervisor could agree in total to a worker's list of preferences. Explore with the worker a realistic set of goals compatible with the policies of the centre, the resources at your disposal and the worker's aspirations.

For instance, it may be an integral part of centre policy that all workers attend courses on equal opportunities and on partnership with parents. The question is only of 'when' workers attend the courses and not 'if'. Part of your role as supervisor could be to discuss and try to resolve a worker's reluctance to go on training that is compulsory for all staff.

Explore how workers' preferences for future learning will build on their existing strengths. Support a worker in finding ways to address the weaker points in her practice as identified during supervision. Through guided conversation, you and the worker will define realistic goals which are motivating to this individual worker.

Step three – Possible plans of action to achieve the learning goals
Discuss with the worker a number of possibilities that could enable him or her to work towards the goal(s). It is certainly not the case that all goals require going on a training programme, though a well-chosen course can be very helpful.

Most learning will take place within the centre. You might be able to use your budget to purchase a useful book or video that would meet this worker's learning needs, especially if you foresee that other centre workers are likely to benefit from the same resource. Perhaps a reorganisation to pair this worker with a more experienced worker might be the most effective approach to achieve learning goals. However, the other worker in question should be consulted, and the implications of any reorganisation considered before a final decision is made.

In cooperation with the worker you need to choose the best option for achieving the current goals. Whatever option is chosen needs to be realistic and to offer an appropriate level of challenge and risk.

Step four – Monitoring the plan and evaluating progress
Part of supervision is to monitor and discuss how the plan of action is unfolding and to what extent activities are achieving learning goals. If this worker attended a training course, then what does she feel she gained from the time? If the worker has been paired with a more experienced worker, then how is this arrangement working out?

Records

Accurate records are part of good supervision. A manager, or other senior worker, can be hard pressed to remember the details of a session without notes. Such notes include key points raised within the session, any decisions made or important reminders given to the individual worker. A record helps continuity between sessions and focuses discussion.

A practical approach can be to make some brief notes either as the supervision session unfolds or at the end. You can use the skill of summarising to bring one part of the session to a close and, with the worker's agreement, make a note. For instance, you might say, 'In your judgement it's time that Peter was referred to the speech therapist. You'd like to be the one to broach this with his mother and we've been through what you'll say. I'll make a note to discuss this with you next time'.

Good practice in keeping records applies equally to supervision notes. These should be specific, with your opinions clearly distinguished from factual information. Your views should be supported by facts. The record should be open to the individual worker and could have a section for that person to add comments.

Supervision of students

The process of supervising students shares many features of staff supervision. An additional element is that supervision has to be closely linked with students' programmes of study. Effective supervision of students on placement will clearly be helped by good working relationships with staff from the college or assessment centre.

Centre workers can only help students' learning when they focus on experiences that students need and the particular skills and knowledge that they expect to gain from this placement. Course tutors should have a good understanding of particular students' strengths and weaknesses. Workers in a centre are in a different position to identify aspects of students' practice in a constructive way.

Reading on . . .

★   Hunt, Nigel 1994: *How to Conduct Staff Appraisals* (How To Books).
★   Morrison, Tony 1993: *Staff Supervision in Social Care : An action learning approach* (Longman).

Stress at work

Working with children and families is hard work. It can be immensely satisfying, but does not offer a soft career option. The work requires commitment that draws on workers' physical, intellectual and emotional resources. Yet, in common with any caring profession, workers have to retain a degree of detachment. There are boundaries to the professional role, and many aspects of children's and families' lives will be outside workers' control.

It is important that workers develop close relationships with children and good working relations with parents. However, the long-term responsibility for the children remains with their families, and parents will make the final decision on many issues. Senior workers need to support their staff in managing the balance between caring and detachment.

Some early years centres cater to families with multiple problems or to children with severe developmental delay or disabilities. Support systems

---

ACTIVITY

Good practice is to seek some feedback from workers about the supervision that you offer. You could ask your staff to answer the following questions (anonymously on paper if they wish).

- In my supervision sessions with you, please tell me what kind of discussions are usually helpful and which are not so useful.
- In supervision what would you like me to do more of?
- What would you like me to do less of?
- Is there anything that you find unhelpful and that I should stop doing?
- What do I get about right?

Look at the answers with an open mind and discuss the patterns with the person who gives you supervision. Identify three practical ways that you could improve the supervision you offer.

within centres are necessary to enable workers to focus on what can be done and how best to proceed. Patience, realism and dealing with frustration effectively can be crucial in such circumstances. Neither children nor families are helped by workers who become disheartened by what they cannot achieve.

Signs of stress

Stress in itself helps us to act and temporary stress is not necessarily dangerous to well-being. In fact, successfully coping with difficulties can be a source of learning and a boost to workers' confidence. It is when pressures continue that stress becomes strain or even distress. Excessive demands on a worker's time, energy and emotional commitment can be seriously draining. Such demands can come from other workers or families, but sometimes individuals compound their own difficulties by being unwilling to ask for support or to delegate to colleagues. Continued stress can damage workers' health and will make them ineffective in their work, perhaps even becoming a risk to the children and families they should be helping.

Physical signs

Continuing fatigue is a warning sign. Everyone gets tired sometimes, but when workers experience continuing stress, it becomes ever more difficult to recoup their energies. A good night's sleep is no longer enough and they become vulnerable to all the minor illnesses that are going around the centre. It is reasonable to expect that workers do not take time off for minor sniffles, but it is in nobody's interest that a sick worker carries on with the insistence of, 'I can take it. I won't let the centre down'. Increased use of over-the-counter medication, in order to get through the day, is also a warning sign.

Psychological signs

Workers under stress do not just become physically ill, their emotions reflect the overload. These may be feelings that, 'It's all too much' or 'What's the point anyway?' Workers under stress may start to look towards inappropriate sources of personal support from the children or demand that parents should be more grateful for the service offered. Emotional strain may also show through mistakes in the work – forgetting something important or failing to concentrate on play with a child. Tears may be close to the surface for no apparent reason and enjoyment with work disappears. People no longer feel they 'want to go' to work, but that they 'have to'.

A combination of serious physical and psychological effects of stress can lead to a downward spiral in which individuals are increasingly unable to cope and become a serious liability to themselves and others.

Coping with stress at work

A positive approach to stress within early years work has several strands:

- An atmosphere has to develop in a centre such that workers feel able to ask for specific help or to talk over concerns in confidence with senior workers. Caring for each other greatly helps workers to care for the children.
- A responsible centre manager is also alert to signs of stress within the team. A key sign is a tendency in workers to see matters as absolutely right or wrong and a general increase in impatience. A good manager reacts sooner rather than later to improve the situation, without assuming that a stressed worker is weak or incompetent.
- Senior workers also need to be aware of signs of stress in themselves, rather than blithely assuming that stress happens to other people. They

should be modelling the kind of behaviour that is part of positive stress management, such as admitting that they need some help. Team members are unlikely to feel they can admit to being overloaded if the manager staggers in with flu or works overly long hours.

- Senior workers can help by showing an ability to delegate work, to assess priorities, rather than desperately trying to do everything at once, and by recognising boundaries to what is possible within the service.
- Finally, the manager should be aware of personal circumstances which may be increasing a worker's stress level. Ideally, this should surface in supervision or general conversation.

 CASE STUDY

Keith has had a hectic year since he took over as manager of Gables Community Nursery. There have been worries about funding and conflict with parents over policy. Within the year, Keith's mother died from cancer. He has avoided talking about his distress to any of his colleagues, although Paranjit has tried to be supportive, having lost her father in the same way.

One of the new developments that he made in Gables was to set up regular supervision for all the workers. Funds do not run to employing an official deputy, so Keith feels he has to cover all the supervision sessions himself. Carla acts as unofficial second-in-line. She has expressed interest in taking on some of the supervision, but Keith has postponed any decision.

His days are so busy that he takes much of the paperwork home and his partner, although very supportive of Keith's taking the job, is now complaining that work dominates their weekends. Keith's answer is to say that things will get better soon, but privately he wonders how soon.

He is beginning to be concerned about his capacity to cope. Recently, he nearly missed the deadline for a grant application and his mind has wandered during some supervision sessions. He is on his third bout of illness in two months, sleeps poorly and finds it hard to get going on Monday mornings.

Question
Keith is dedicated and responsible. His current dilemma does not have a neat solution, yet he cannot safely carry on in this way. Outline possible ways forward to relieve some of the stress on Keith, which would be consistent with offering a good service to families.

Reading on . . .

★ Cooper, Cary L., Cooper, Rachel D. and Eaker, Lynn H. 1988: *Living with Stress* (Penguin Books).
★ Cranwell-Ward, Jane 1987: *Managing Stress* (Pan Books).

4.3 Staff development

Planned professional development
Using internal resources

The resources within a centre can be tapped by workers' being prepared to learn from one another and to share their skills and knowledge. For instance:

- Some flexibility of roles within a centre enables workers to add to their skills. This pattern only works well if time is given to explain unfamiliar tasks in the new role. (See 'delegation' on page 32.)
- Pairing junior and senior workers can work well, so long as the more experienced worker has a sound grasp of the process of coaching (see page 91) and the less experienced worker respects the colleague's skills and knowledge.
- Supervision sessions can be used to plan new learning and to reflect upon what has been learned.
- Sometimes workers can explore through individual study – reading or using other resources such as video.

External resources

Daily experience can be complemented by attendance on training courses. Your local authority may offer relevant short courses and national early years organisations often organise conferences and workshops. You will need to choose courses that will develop staff skills and be feasible within your budget. The benefits of a course can be extended if workers are expected to present key points at a team meeting afterwards.

Releasing staff for longer courses will require more organisation but can benefit both the worker and the centre. This book supports in particular the NVQs and SVQs in Child Care and Education but members of staff who do not work directly with children may be interested in other NVQs. Assessment within the S/NVQ framework is based on competence in the place of work and evidence of such competence can be submitted in several different ways. In order for your staff to benefit from S/NVQs, your centre has to be accepted as an approved assessment centre in its own right or be part of a consortium. As a manager, consider qualifying as a workplace assessor because you would then be able to assess the competence of your own workers who have registered for S/NVQs.

For further information

Contact the National Council for Vocational Qualifications (NCVQ) who will provide information about current S/NVQs and those being developed, and will put you in contact with the relevant awarding body.

★ NCVQ, 222 Euston Road, London NW1 2BZ *(tel*: 0171 387 9898).

A positive outlook

The support of colleagues is vital to help workers to continue to learn, but a lot depends on individual workers themselves:

- A willingness to continue to learn is crucial. It is an irresponsible worker who takes the approach, 'I've done my basic training, so that's it'.
- Workers need to be willing to reflect on their practice and acknowledge that an area in which they could learn more is *not* proof of failure.
- Workers need to ask for feedback on their current practice from a supervisor or colleagues and to express their hopes and aspirations.
- Workers have to be willing to stretch themselves both to learn new skills and to practice until they become more confident. Some individuals may find this type of risk-taking harder to tolerate. (The 'risk' here is of not managing as well as the worker would hope; risks should never be taken with children's safety or well-being.)

Dealing with mistakes

It is inevitable that workers will make mistakes. It may be some time before it becomes obvious that a particular approach was, with hindsight, not the best option. Adults and children will benefit from an atmosphere in which mistakes are assumed to be the result of misunderstanding or poor communication rather than malevolent intent. Mistakes should be handled with consideration rather than mocking or anger. Most mistakes, after all, are unintentional or the unexpected consequence of good intentions. Part of the role of senior workers is to monitor work so that mistakes do not go undetected, and to ensure that practice is in line with policy.

If you have made a mistake, then it is important to acknowledge the error, even if you feel foolish or irritated with yourself. Give yourself some thinking time to consider what you could learn from the experience and ask for specific guidance from your supervisor if that would help.

If you are providing supervision, you can help in a number of ways:

- Support workers in talking about what has happened and discussing their feelings. Admitting to a mistake is an important step, but endlessly going over old ground may block learning. Focus on what can be done and not on why the mistake should not have happened.
- Talk with workers about what they can learn to improve their practice for the future. What do they recognise that they did not know or understand? Are there skills that they could usefully improve?
- Alert workers if they are being unduly harsh on themselves. Sometimes a worker may have made the best decision, given the information available at the time. Some workers hold impossible standards of perfection for themselves and this can lead to serious stress.
- Be ready to identify any broader issues that may arise. For instance, has an atmosphere developed in the centre in which workers are loath to ask for help or admit that they do not know something?

Not all errors can be dealt with through discussion. Serious mistakes that led to potential or actual risk to a child would almost certainly have to be written up as a report. Errors of judgement that affected families have to be documented, if parents wish to lodge a formal complaint.

The process of coaching

Previously, the term 'coaching' was used only for sports training, but it has been used increasingly to mean guided support in a wide array of professions. The advantage of the term is that it focuses on learning by doing, not just by passively listening and writing notes. Coaching typically consists of a series

TO THINK ABOUT

There is continuity between how workers treat each other within a centre and their approach to the children. If workers feel that mistakes are failures and nothing can be learned except to cover up the error, they are unlikely to be positive about children's mistakes. In a similar way, a group of workers who feels neither valued nor encouraged is unlikely to offer a positive environment in which children can learn.

of one-to-one meetings, with an agreement on the actions to be undertaken between each meeting in order to achieve defined learning of skills.

Preparing to coach

Through coaching, you work to transfer your own competencies to another person who has less experience, understanding or knowledge. Effective coaching is a subtle blend of sharing what you know and can do with allowing the other person to develop skills within their own style and to practise at their own pace.

You will not be effective in coaching unless you are fully aware of how you carry out this area of responsibility. It will be helpful if you prepare by thinking about the following issues:

- What do I do and what are my reasons for carrying out the task in this way?
- How can I break down this task into identifiable and manageable steps?
- Is there a logical pattern to how this work should be undertaken? If so, how can I explain it?
- What was it like not to know how to carry out this part of my work? (It can help immensely if you recapture what it felt like to you before this area of skill became more automatic to you.)

What can seem very obvious or 'just common sense' to an experienced worker can be utterly confusing to someone who is at the early stage of learning.

The learning task

A good coach offers:

- manageable steps to challenge but not to overwhelm;
- supported practice, with moderate pressure to learn;
- encouragement, patience and constructive feedback;
- regular meetings to review progress and set new steps.

Using a series of meetings – not necessarily very long – coaching follows several practical steps.

1 Agree on the task
The ideal focus for coaching is for a less experienced worker to complete a task that you have delegated, with plenty of opportunity to talk with you, so that the task can be fully understood and properly undertaken. The task should be something within the worker's remit that she is motivated to learn or definitely needs to understand.

CASE STUDY

Moira, the assistant in Farm Road Nursery Class, wanted to 'work more closely with parents'. In discussion with Carole (the nursery teacher) Moira focused on questions from parents about why the nursery 'isn't doing anything about reading and writing'. Moira wanted to organise a meeting for parents that would explain how the work in the nursery builds the basis for reading and writing. Moira's goal was to plan and organise the meeting this term.

Carole encouraged Moira to voice all her ideas for the parents' meeting and follow through how any of the potential plans could be put into action. Moira had initially thought of an evening meeting, but had not anticipated baby-sitting problems for families. Carole shared her experience of organising an evening meeting at short notice and with no crèche: a mistake that taught her about the complexities of family life. They followed through the pros and cons of different kinds of meetings and informative displays.

Moira agreed that, before they talked again the following Friday, she would draft her ideas for a relevant display and the key points to communicate to parents.

1 Think through the other issues that will have to be covered in later conversations between Carole and Moira.
2 Apply the steps of coaching to a task that you are helping a worker to learn. Check on whether you are using the situation to the full potential, for instance, are you creating the opportunity for safe practice rather than continuing to tell the other person?

2 Encourage self-learning

From your own experience, you can give support and relevant information, but your aim is that the other person does the task.

● Listen actively to the other person's ideas and plans. Reflect back and summarise. Avoid simply telling her; help her to find out for herself.
● Help her to follow through the consequences of any possible lines of action. Ask open-ended questions. Avoid negative reactions such as, 'That won't work' or 'The management committee will be after you if you do that'. If you have reservations, then offer an explanation.

Problems need to be resolved – but in a constructive way

● Share your experience without letting it overwhelm the discussion. Sometimes it will be appropriate to share what you learned from a mistake.

3 Set limits

Part of coaching is to agree with the other person exactly how far she or he will proceed with the task before you meet again. For instance, you decide with the worker whom you are coaching that he will have done all the agreed fact-finding for the centre's annual outing and will come next Tuesday with a detailed budget, but he will not have booked anything yet. Summarise each meeting to make sure that you both have the same understanding of what is to happen before the next one.

Once you have delegated a worker to carry out part of the task then you should not hover over him, checking or nagging. You have cleared the way for him to be visibly responsible for specific tasks, and not beyond.

4 Tell others

Inform other workers that you have given this task to the worker in question. You want colleagues to support the worker and acknowledge that he is learning to complete this task.

Reading on . . .

★ *The Helping Hand: Coaching skills for managers* (Video Arts booklet).

4.4 Confronting poor standards in work

At some point, managers have to deal with work standards which are lower than they require for the centre. You may tackle the poor work of an individual, or the insistence of several workers to flout centre policy. Such situations have to be confronted in an assertive way. This section deals specifically with the discipline interview and disciplinary procedures. You will also find page 110 useful for dealing with angry workers.

The discipline interview

The objective of interviewing a worker whose practice is unsatisfactory is to close the gap between what would be an acceptable standard of behaviour and the current situation. A discipline interview will not be productive if you use it solely to reprimand the worker. The objective is to improve standards.

You will have feelings about the prospect of the discipline interview, and so will the worker(s) involved. You need to recognise what you are feeling; it may be frustration or anger as well as anxiety about confronting the worker. For the interview, put your feelings to one side and use your skills to focus on the exchange as a fact-finding exercise. The interview is business-like and formal, with the manager in control.

- Check the facts both before you meet the worker and by questions during the interview. Use this information to show the gap between what you expect this worker to do and what is happening in practice.
- Explore the reasons for this gap. Ask open-ended questions and *listen* to what the worker has to say. If necessary, tolerate silences until the worker replies. Avoid jumping to conclusions or taking another worker's view as the whole truth.
- Agree a plan of action to close the gap. Explore and seek commitment from the worker about what she will do, by when and in what way. Explain the consequences if she does not keep her commitment. If it is appropriate to take action yourself, then commit to what and when. Write down the agreement you have reached and give the worker a copy. Agree a time to meet again in the near future.

Write up your notes after the interview and plan to tackle any more general issues that have been raised. Perhaps the discussion has revealed a long-standing difficulty between this worker and her colleague in the room. Assign yourself thinking time and a specific date by which you will deal with this issue.

Grievance and disciplinary procedures

Sometimes a conflict may not be resolved, despite the efforts of those involved. As such, a centre has to have formal procedures for dealing with such problems. Some procedures are determined by legislation on employment (check the books suggested on page 81 and at the end of this section).

- Grievance procedures are for paid staff or voluntary workers to pursue issues such as conditions of service, management support or behaviour.
- Disciplinary procedures are started when a worker has failed to comply with codes of conduct in the centre, with specific instructions over the work or has behaved unprofessionally.

(These two procedures should not be confused with the centre's complaints procedure, since the latter is for service users – see page 113.)

The process followed in these procedures should be open and clear. It will be the choice of workers to initiate grievance procedures, as it is the option of parents or other users of the centre to make a formal complaint. It is not the role of centre manager either to encourage or to dissuade someone from starting the process. You should provide the necessary paperwork and explain the steps of the procedure, if the other person seems unclear.

A manager should never deal *alone* with any disciplinary action or grievance procedure. As soon as it becomes clear that procedures will be needed, you should inform and consult appropriately. In some centres this will mean contacting your line management within social services or education. In a private nursery you should talk with the owner; in other centres you inform the chair of the management committee.

Disciplinary procedures

These procedures should never be started lightly, nor should the prospect be used as a threat against a worker or volunteer. However, certain kinds of behaviour cannot be ignored. It is a serious matter if workers neglect their responsibilities to the children or endanger their well-being. It is unacceptable for any worker to contravene the policies of the centre, for instance on handling children's behaviour or anti-racist practice.

In most cases, a manager needs to show that efforts have been made to influence a worker towards the required good practice (see 'The discipline interview'). Part of the disciplinary process is one or more formal warnings, at least one in writing. Check your own procedures for details and any circumstances that justify the immediate suspension of a worker.

If you are seriously concerned about the behaviour and standards of a worker in your centre, you should keep written records before the situation reaches formal proceedings.

- Treat the records as potentially open to the worker and to the committee that would handle any disciplinary action.
- Make sure notes are clearly factual, with dates and times of what happened, what was said and any instructions that were given to the worker.
- Make sure that any opinions are supported. You must show evidence of observation.

Sometimes evidence for a disciplinary action may arise from a formal complaint from a parent. The two processes should be kept separate in that both must be handled in line with the correct procedures and seen to be resolved one way or another. At some point, the complaint from the parent will become part of the information that has to be considered in the disciplinary process.

Reading on . . .

★ Markham, Ursula 1993: *How to Deal with Difficult People* (Thorsons).
★ *I'd Like a Word with You: The discipline interview* (Video Arts booklet).

ACTIVITY

Look carefully at the grievance and disciplinary procedures for your centre.

- Are the steps in the process clear to you? If not, then consult your line management or the management committee of the centre.
- Is it clear what kind of behaviour on the part of workers could be cause for disciplinary action? Again, consult if the circumstances are vague.

5 Partnership with parents

This chapter covers:

- partnership in practice;
- positive relationships between parents and workers;
- dealing with complaints.

5.1 Partnership in practice

The outlook of workers

Genuine partnership will depend on the attitudes towards parents shown through workers' behaviour.

- Workers must have respect for parents as the people with the long-term responsibility for their children. It is understandable that workers wish for appreciation of their skills but focus must be a mutual respect of different expertise.

To be of value, ideas have to be put into practice

- Centres offer a service to children and their families and, even in areas where families have little choice, workers should avoid any sense of 'parents should just be grateful'.
- Workers should be willing to look from parents' perspective and not just from their own priorities. This alternative perspective includes differences in cultural tradition or religious beliefs.
- Communication should be an open and honest two-way exchange of views and never a one-way 'I am the expert' telling from workers.
- Centre staff should make the effort to support and empower parents, never to undermine or belittle their status.

The relationship will not always be between workers and parents. Some children may be cared for by grandparents or other relatives. Sessional groups may find that they see little of working parents and need to build a relationship with the children's childminder or nanny.

Workers should keep a flexible view on the shape of families. Some children will be living with two parents, although both adults will not always be the child's birth parents. Some families are run by lone parents, usually but not always the mother. Most parents are heterosexual, but some children live with lesbian mothers or gay fathers, perhaps also with their partners.

Reading on . . .

★ De'Ath, Erica 1991: *Changing Families: A guide for early years workers* (National Early Years Network).

The perspective of parents

The partnership between workers and parents will also be shaped by the parents' views. Some may be wary of the expertise of workers; others may feel confident of their own abilities as a parent. All workers need to be aware that individual parents may have very different perceptions of the work of the centre and the involvement of early years workers with their children.

When there is limited choice

Discussion about early years provision often assumes that parents can choose between possible settings to suit them and their child. Although some families have a choice, in many parts of the country there may be only one local under-fives setting or one type of provision. The national distribution is even more unequal for after-school and holiday care for the 5–8s. Under these circumstances, partnership remains very important, but appreciate that parents' outlook will be shaped by awareness that there is no real alternative. For instance, they may be loath to voice any criticism of the centre.

Children and family centres have to manage a relationship with parents that may begin with feelings of duress. Families may be referred to the centre by health visitors or social workers who press parents to take up the place for the well-being of their children. Parents involved with the child protection team may have little choice about accepting the place for their child and perhaps attending themselves as well.

Reading on . . .

For the perspective of parents seeking pre-school provision or child care see:
★ Lindon, Jennie 1996: 'Care and experience outside the family' in *The Good Housekeeping Complete Book of Parenting* (Ebury Press).

Whose centre is it?
To a greater or lesser extent, all parents will be sensitive that they and their children are entering someone else's 'territory'. The most welcoming early-years setting is still a place whose ground rules are determined by people other than just the parents. Parents and children may be involved in a range of decisions, but the centre is still not the family home. Parents feel, and genuinely are, less in control.

 CASE STUDY

In Salmon Lane Private Nursery, Debbie has worked hard to encourage her staff to recognise that how they behave affects their relationship with parents. When she started, there had been a lot of comments like, 'Parents should be grateful; lots of people can't find any child care round here' and an approach of 'They should say "Hello" first, why does it always have to be us?'.

Debbie avoided any fault-finding and stressed that workers had a professional obligation to look at their own actions. It was part of their job description that they work in partnership with parents.

Slowly, workers noticed that friendly overtures to even the quieter parents were met with pleasure. One mother explained how, 'I never used to stay and talk about Chris's day because I always got the feeling I was under your feet'. Debbie addressed the skills of dealing with angry parents through discussion in team meetings and sending two workers on a relevant course. Debbie then arranged an individual session with the most argumentative worker on the team and laid out very firmly that certain kinds of behaviour towards parents were unacceptable.

Question
The concept in the case study is that people only have direct influence over their own behaviour. Workers cannot directly control what parents do, but can set a positive trend through their own actions. Describe two applications of this idea in your own setting.

Agreements between centre and parents

Partnership has to include a shared understanding of the service – what the providers of a service are offering and what in turn is expected of the users. A well-worded agreement, within the context of open communication, can help to manage expectations about the boundaries to a service.

Commitment from parents
A written agreement between the centre and parent(s) should cover the most important details without becoming a lengthy item of paperwork. Usually, the following is included:

- The details of the place offered to the child(ren) – the number of sessions or days and times.
- Payment – how much, when fees should be paid and the consequences of non-payment; whether fees are due when a child is ill or on holiday; any other costs that will be extra, for instance, swimming trips.
- Notice to the effect that the centre does not care for children when they are sick and would expect parents to fetch them in the event of illness or accident.
- Conditions for ending a place – the period of notice from either the centre or parents; circumstances when the centre would review or withdraw a child's place.
- The centre's complaints procedure.
- Permissions for local outings. Other trips would require specific permission from parents.

Inequitable agreements will not work

An agreement will probably end with a phrase such as, 'I have read the conditions of the place for my child(ren) – names – and agree to carry out my responsibilities as described'. Parent(s) sign and date the agreement, which should also be signed by a senior worker. Although these agreements are sometimes called 'contracts', they are not legal documents.

It would be very unwise to attempt to cover everything in a written agreement. Future contact offers opportunities to explore misunderstandings or inaccurate expectations on *both* sides.

Rights and responsibilities
A useful and workable agreement, even an informal one, has to cover the rights and responsibilities of both parties. A written agreement, such as outlined above, will not cover all the obligations of the centre. You would explain what you offer to children and families through conversation and giving parents a copy of your main policies.

As soon as you write down the rights of any individual or group, you are also making a statement about someone else's responsibilities. For instance, the centre has established its right to be paid for the service, but with this

ACTIVITY

Parents will not be impressed by an uneven agreement that pins them down to very specific promises about times and payment of fees, but only expresses the centre's commitment to the family as a vague 'we'll do our best'.

● If your centre has a written agreement, then look carefully at the detail to judge whether the promises asked of parents and the commitments you are offering are equally specific. Consider also what you say to parents who are seeking a place for their child.

A key question to ask is 'How easily can we tell if promises are kept?' You cannot easily judge failure to 'do our best', because the promise is so vague.

If your centre does not have its own written agreement, then look at the agreement issued by any other centre or perhaps the local primary or secondary school. Analyse the details in the same way.

● Use what you have learned to draft a fair agreement for your own centre and to plan what you say in conversation with parents.

right comes a responsibility to run efficient accounts. Parents have the right to expect that their payments are entered promptly and that they are not chased for money they have already paid. Parents who keep their promise to pay the fees are likely to get angry if other families are allowed to fall into arrears without any penalty.

Reviewing agreements

Agreements should be regularly reviewed. There are two ways in which you might undertake this evaluation:

1   As with any part of your practice, you should discuss, from time to time, whether the type of agreement used in the centre appears to be working. If not, what are the main sources of difficulty?
2   Children and family centres are likely to undertake specific programmes of work with parents and children. Any agreements with parents should include a date when workers and parents will meet to discuss the outcome of the agreement and to set further goals if appropriate (see page 27).

Partnership and information

Genuine partnership cannot exist without equality in the partners' access to information. This process starts during the first meeting between parents and workers, when the parents are given a clear picture of how the centre operates. Continued communication has to be both informative and respond to parents' individual queries. Good practice in your centre over the twin issues of access and confidentiality will build an atmosphere of trust, in which parents are far more likely to tell workers of family issues and crises which could affect the child. Parents who fear centre gossip will not share personal concerns. (See Chapter 1 for further discussion of these issues.)

Shared responsibility

Children spend only some of their waking hours at early years settings. Another aspect of partnership is to build continuity between what happens in the centre and in the child's own home. The two experiences do not have to be identical. Parents may want their children to attend playgroup or nursery school precisely because the activities contrast with possibilities at home. Each has a complementary part to play in children's development.

Shared care

Continuity can be an especially important issue in centres which have very young children and which offer full day care. Workers and parents need to have regular conversations about developments such as weaning babies or when to start toilet training. Workers should not simply impose their opinions. Parents will have views, for instance, about the move to solid foods and some preferences will be influenced by cultural or religious traditions.

There should be prompt communication about children's health and well-being. Parents need to explain carefully to workers about a child's continuing health condition or the impact of a disability. Workers should recognise that some parents will be knowledgeable about a condition, if it specifically affects their own child. Parents should always be consulted about referral to specialists, even if these professionals visit the centre on a regular basis.

You need to tell parents if children have become unwell during the day and also have a clear centre policy about the circumstances under which parents would be called to collect their child. Babies can become ill very swiftly, so it is crucial to exchange information promptly about their health.

During a 'drop-in' morning it may be understood that parents remain responsible for their children

Reading on . . .

Action for Sick Children has two publications which raise awareness about shared health care. Both are written by Mary Slater:

★ 1993: *Health Care for All our Children: Achieving appropriate health care for black and minority ethnic children and their families.*
★ 1995: *Caring for All our Children: A training pack in multi-cultural health care for providers.*

Who is responsible and when?

In any centre there can be awkward times when it is not entirely clear who is primarily responsible for a child. Some examples are:

● *At the beginning and end of a day or a session* At these cross-over times it may be uncertain whether responsibility has passed between parents and workers. You may be able to mark the moment by saying, 'Bijal, your Mummy's here. You go with her now'. But, everyone has to be clear this means that the parent now has responsibility. When parent and child are in dispute, a worker's most useful contribution can be to remove the interested audience of other children. Depending on the exact situation and your relationship with the parent, you may or may not get involved. Or, you might say later, 'Mark was a little so-and-so about putting on his coat. I didn't want to interfere, but another time, would you like some help?'

● *On trips out with parents as extra helpers* Special trips may not be possible unless parents boost the adult–child ratio. Make it clear which adults have responsibility for which children and that this obligation lasts for the length of the trip. Check on the terms of your insurance for personal injury; parents may not be able to take responsibility for children other than their own.

● *When parents are present in the group* Parents may be involved in helping to run the group, perhaps on a rota basis. This type of parental involvement needs careful planning (see page 120). In children and family centres part of the work may require parents to attend some days. So, both the parent and worker can be in the same room and the adults have to work out who will primarily relate to the child, who will do the reprimanding and other issues.

In any of the examples the situation has to be made clear, and sometimes issues defused, through communication between the adults. Confusion over responsibility can create nothing more than irritation, but in some circumstances there could be real danger to the child's safety. Children take opportunities to play one adult off against another. It is the adults' responsibility to resolve this situation and not simply to blame the child.

Children may play adults against each other – it is the adults' responsibility to sort this out amicably

Decisions

Partnership is not a continuously equal relationship in that every decision is 50–50. The balance will shift, depending on the circumstances.

Any decisions made in the centre have to allow for obligations to all the children and families who attend, as well as the policies and agreed procedures. You should listen to parents' views and the decisions that they would prefer to take. Sometimes, a parent's line of argument might show an important, alternative perspective that shifts practice in the centre. Good practice would never be to assume, 'we must be right, we're the professionals!'

Parents are primary decision-makers for their own children and have to live with the consequences of their own decisions. Workers may not always agree, and may work hard to persuade a parent, for instance about the importance of good dental care or about not delaying a decision about primary schools to the very last moment. However, the final decision rests with the parent.

TO THINK ABOUT

In a real sense, the majority of the customers of the centre are parents. The centre depends on offering a service that satisfies them. It is central to effective relationships to treat parents as you would wish to be treated as a valued customer.

5.2 Positive relationships with parents

Friendly but not friends

Partnership with parents is a working relationship. You may be on friendly terms with many of the parents but you are not starting a personal friendship. Some workers have difficulty in practice with the distinction between a friendly relationship and becoming friends.

Parents and workers have met because of the children and their development and welfare must be a primary consideration. However well you get along with parents you cannot guarantee to behave towards them in the way that a friend would react. For instance, a friend might drop all other obligations to help out or would promise to keep all confidences secret. Workers can offer *neither* of these commitments. Your responsibilities to other families cannot be pushed aside. Furthermore, you are obliged to report some confidences, particularly those that imply possible risk to the child.

Such problems can be worsened when the boundaries between work and personal life have become unclear. Workers have a right to a private life, but some circumstances may undermine professional objectivity. A manager needs to support workers who experience difficulties in saying 'No' to requests. A manager should challenge workers who behave differently towards parents according to whether they like the parent or not.

TO THINK ABOUT

Please look at each of the following examples and note down the main issues involved.

- A worker baby-sits regularly for two families whose children attend the centre.
- A boy who attended the centre has died. His mother has written with details of the funeral, inviting staff to attend the service.
- A worker was school friends with one of the parents. During a staff break, he entertains colleagues with tales of the practical jokes they used to play on their teachers.
- A parent has invited all the staff to a party at her house. (Would you judge this example any differently if the centre had organised social events for parents as part of its parent involvement programme?)
- A child has gone into hospital to have her appendix removed. Her key worker plans to visit the child in hospital.
- Over the weekend, one of the female workers is seen at the local cinema with the father of a child who attends the centre.
- One worker attends the same church as several of the parents. Their conversations in the centre sometimes include church business.

1 Which examples are an appropriate form of involvement with families? Is there any element on which a manager should seek reassurance?
2 Where you feel the worker is behaving inappropriately, what steps should be taken by a senior worker?

The beginning of the relationship

Your relationship often starts when parents visit your centre to decide whether they want their child to attend. Where parents have little choice over early years provision, or if they are confident of a recommendation from another parent, then the beginning may be your admissions process.

Centres should have clear procedures about admissions and a fair policy (see page 19). However, the other side of admissions is a personal process. Parents form their first impressions of you, just as much as you do of them. They may appreciate a well-presented centre brochure, but many parents will also want you to talk them through the service offered. Parents want replies to the questions they choose to ask, not just replies to queries put by other parents.

Although you may have gone through this process many times, each parent deserves to be treated as an individual. It must not show that this is the umpteenth time you have explained why the centre asks about a family's religious and ethnic background. This parent should receive the message, by word and body language, that her questions merit an explanation.

Once you get to know parents, they can be a useful source of information about your admissions process. You might find, through informal conversation, that several parents offer a similar, 'I really didn't understand what you meant about ...' or 'You told me so much; I couldn't remember the half of it'. Perhaps you have placed too much emphasis on saying everything in the first meeting and are not allowing for follow-up conversations. Similarly you may learn that some workers are perceived as more friendly than others.

Using names

At the first meeting you will find out the child's name and that of the parents. Children and family centres will take referrals through other professionals such as social workers. In that case, this information may reach you through a letter or report. Check the spelling and pronunciation of all the family names when you meet and make sure you have them right.

People's names are an important part of their identity and several practical issues arise:

- Some children will not share the surname of the parent whom you meet, so it is important to check rather than assume.
- It is better to refer to 'first name' and 'family name' or 'surname'. The term 'Christian name' is only common in Britain because the society has been influenced by the Christian faith. The term is inappropriate for those who follow other faiths or who choose not to follow any religion.
- Children should be called by their own name, with no changes or abbreviations, unless they wish otherwise. The same is true for parents. Early years centres are often informal and workers are known by their first name. Parents may be happy to be addressed in this way, but workers should check this and respect a preference to be addressed by title and surname.
- The Western European naming system is that the personal name comes first, followed by any other personal names and then the shared family surname. All cultures do *not* follow this pattern – neither the order, nor in having a shared surname.

CASE STUDY

Mount Park Children's Centre is situated in a city area with a diverse population. Over a dozen ethnic and cultural groups are represented in the centre. After some embarrassing mistakes about names, Leela drafted a handout for the team. The basic message was, 'Don't assume. Check!' Two specific examples given were:

- Chinese custom is that the surname comes first, followed by a name indicating the generation to which this individual belongs and then the personal name.
- Some Sikhs choose a family name to work as a surname. Devout families do not use surnames; they were abandoned to promote equality since they derived from the caste system. Some Sikh families use the religious titles of Singh (males only) and Kaur (females only) as last names.

Mistakes over naming are an example of how easy it can be to assume that one's own traditions are universal.

1 Note down any other naming traditions that you have encountered personally or from the experience of your team.
2 Use this example to generate further discussion about how what is 'normal' to one cultural, ethnic or religious group is 'unusual' to others.

Workers and parents are getting to know each other

Settling children

At the first meeting with parents, a period for settling children should be discussed and a provisional plan agreed. You cannot be rigid in this since children vary considerably. Some wave goodbye without a backward glance, whereas others like the play but are loath to allow their parent to leave. Parents will also have other obligations – to their job or to other children. An uncompromising time period of settling in might place serious burdens on them.

It will not always be a parent who settles children into the centre. Some children may be cared for by grandparents or other relatives. In other families, it may be the child's minder or nanny who eases the first few days and she may then be the main link between centre and family. (In this chapter please read 'parent' as 'parent or other carer'.)

In most centres children will be staying without their parent once they are settled. Drop-in parents' clubs may require parents to stay and remain responsible for their children. A settling-in pattern could have the aim of helping parent and child to separate for parts of the session.

After-school clubs or holiday schemes that cater for over-fives are likely to run a different settling-in process. Good contact with parents will be important, probably through the first meeting, but it is less likely that workers will suggest, or that children will want, a parent to stay. The invitation to parents to have a cup of tea and watch the play activities if they wish will probably be the most suitable solution.

Children's feelings

Through the settling process, you might reasonably hope for a happy child who allows her parent to leave. However, some children are still distressed, even if great care has been taken in easing them into the centre's day or session.

Children may want to stay close until they feel more settled

You should discuss the situation with a parent if a child is very resistant to the parent's leaving. Together, you need to plan separation by stages and to accept that, however hard you both try, this child may still cry. Reassure parents that they will be contacted if their child remains inconsolable.

Any difficulties need to be explored through conversation and with sensitivity to the feelings of parent and child. It would be poor practice to

---

 CASE STUDY

Carole, the teacher, and Moira, her assistant, decided to review the settling-in process at Farm Road Nursery Class. The previous teacher set up a compulsory pattern of short periods of time initially, building up to the whole session after a minimum of a week.

Carole and Moira's first step was to have an informal conversation with parents whose children had been in the nursery for at least three months. The workers asked the same question, 'Looking back on when you settled (name of child) into the nursery, how do you think we could have made those days better for you both?'

Some parents said the settling time was fine; others made comments:

- 'I really didn't know what you wanted me to do. You just said I'd got to be in the nursery with Laura. I enjoyed helping at the water tray, but I wasn't sure that I was supposed to play with other people's children too.'

- 'I thought Jessie was ready for me to leave on the first day. After all, she knew the nursery from coming with her elder brother. She couldn't wait to get in here. But you wouldn't let me go till I'd done my time.'

- 'I was pleased when you suggested I should go, even though we both knew Jamal was going to cry. I think I could've stayed for weeks and he would still have been upset when I left.'

- 'I wish you'd introduced yourselves properly. There were two other parents in with me and Tom. I thought one of them was a teacher.'

1   What main points should Carole and Moira take from the parents' comments? How could they plan a better settling-in process?

2   Have you asked for feedback about settling-in from parents in your centre? If yes, what were the main issues they suggested? If no, then try some open-ended questions.

become irritated with a child or to dismiss their strong emotions as 'clinging'. Likewise, if a child calms and stops crying after the parent has gone, it does not prove that the tears were just for attention. The feelings are genuine and the calmness may be from resignation, or the distracting quality of play.

The feelings of parents

Parents have mixed feelings about the process. Many experience an uncomfortable blend of wishing their child to be content, yet do not really want a situation in which the child scarcely seems to notice when a parent leaves. Grandparents, minders or nannies who take responsibility for child care, may experience the same feelings.

Workers should respect these feelings and try to understand them. Parents who need child care to allow them to work may genuinely not be able to stay long to settle their child. There may be pressure on them from unsympathetic employers and the settling time may have be taken as unpaid leave.

Parents need guidance on how they are expected to behave when they are settling their child in. For instance, they may wonder if they are supposed to stay close to their child or make active attempts to withdraw. A few suggestions can help parents feel more comfortable, as the case study shows.

Reading on . . .

★ The Pre-school Learning Alliance publishes leaflets for staff and parents on *Settling at playgroup*, *Helping at playgroup* and other practical issues. You will find the leaflets helpful whether you work in a playgroup or are drafting your own material for a different type of centre.

Good communication
A welcome to parents

A partnership is a relationship and relationships need attention, hence all centres need regular communication with parents. These exchanges do not have to be about something significant. Good relations can be built through friendly contact that brings worker and parent together as adults. Just chatting is positive.

If parents feel that nobody notices if they are there or not, they will be disinclined to think of the centre as a place in which they could become involved. If parents who stay during the day or play session do not feel that they are made genuinely welcome, then they will not bother to stay again.

Workers are responsible for ensuring that parents who already attend also make new arrivals welcome. If established parents and workers give the impression of being a self-sufficient clique, then parents who are new may feel excluded.

Part of a warm welcome is for parents to see people like themselves and their children reflected in centre displays and play materials. Displays that reflect only some of the families, their culture and background are giving a covert message that the centre prefers and values those groups.

Managing conversations

It can be difficult to have long conversations, especially in centres where all the parents are concentrated into the same span of time at the beginning and end of the day or session. Parents who do not have paid jobs may be happy to linger, but they too will have other obligations. Centres offering day care

It is important to find the time for conversation

or after-school care can face an influx of parents, tired after work and knowing they still have domestic obligations when they get home.

Even in a busy day or session it should be possible to acknowledge parents with a wave or a smile and sometimes, perhaps not every day, a short conversation. It is important to monitor yourself to check that you are not only speaking to those parents with whom you feel at ease. The manager should encourage this review from staff. It is important that exchanges with parents are not only started when there is some worry about children or if they have misbehaved during the day. Workers should make the effort to share with parents what activities children have enjoyed during the day.

Centres ideally need a room in which a worker and parent can talk in privacy when the conversation is more confidential. The manager has to organise how this will be managed.

When communication may be difficult

Disabilities of hearing or speech

Perhaps you have some degree of hearing loss. If so, tell parents so they can take practical steps, such as making sure that they face you and that their words are as clear as possible. Parents may be more ready to repeat a comment, knowing that you are interested but may have lost some of the meaning with all the background noise of the centre. If you do not tell them, parents might conclude that your not replying was inattention or rudeness.

Sometimes parents have disabilities of hearing or of speech that lead to difficulties for other people in understanding what they say. The best way forward will depend on the individual parent. For instance:

- If someone can lip-read then they need to see other people's faces. Full face contact signals that this particular communication is for this parent. In a busy centre, the direction of communication is not always obvious.
- All workers need to know that a particular parent cannot, for instance, hear a call from a distance and will not respond unless she can see the message of a wave or a beckon.
- Some, but not all, adults with hearing loss use sign language. If no workers can sign, then ideally arrange for someone to learn. Writing may act as the best short-term answer.
- Some parents may have a stutter that interrupts the fluency of their speech. This difficulty is likely to become worse if they feel rushed. You can help by showing no signs of being in a hurry and do not rush to finish parents' sentences for them.
- Perhaps a parent with a disability of hearing or speech will find communication easier through a hearing friend. If you are involved in this kind of three-way conversation, then it is important to share your attention between the parent and the friend. It would be very discourteous to look only at the speaking adult or to refer to the parent as 'she'.

You do not share a language

In some centres, parents and workers are bilingual. Several practical issues arise if adults do not share a language to the same level of fluency:

- Your spoken communication should be direct and simple. It is possible to express requests and ideas in short sentences, conveying one point at a time. Be prepared also to express your message in more than one way.
- Support spoken communication with written material (brochures about the centre or letters to parents) in the family's language.
- Workers can learn at least some phrases in the family's language, for instance, courtesy expressions for greeting or thanks.

Children's drawings can reflect the good relationship made with a worker

● Look for any opportunities to employ bilingual workers or support your current workers who are motivated to learn another language.

If you speak a second language, you will appreciate that the level of knowledge that works well in activities such as shopping does not easily stretch to discussing child development. So, even parents who are bilingual still appreciate efforts towards straightforward English.

The end of the relationship

Some centres have a relationship with families stretching over years but, even in those circumstances, children and parents will move on in the end. There are tremendous benefits in having a happy working relationship with parents and children. Yet, the cost that everyone pays is sadness when the relationship has to end. Workers are often sad when children leave and the children may be distressed when they have to say goodbye. The end of the relationship also affects parents, who may regret the passing of an era.

Involvement in the centre can be an important part of a parent's life. Friends may have been made in the parents' group. Or, a parent may have gained confidence as a regular helper and will be uncertain how to use these skills elsewhere. A responsible manager will have guidelines for parents who wish to continue helping in the group once their child has moved on. Centres could also gather practical information on other voluntary work or the possibilities in further training. If your work is as much with parents as children, then part of your task will be to encourage parents away from dependence on the centre and ease their transition to the next stage.

Of course, there is not always sadness. Some children are ready to move on and their excitement about the next stage outweighs any preference for staying in familiar surroundings. Some workers are relieved to see the back of particular children and parents. It is not appropriate to show this relief and all families deserve a courteous goodbye, whatever the previous relationship has been. Parents may sometimes be pleased to have their child move on from a centre in which they were dissatisfied or from workers whom they disliked.

5.3 Dealing with complaints

Dissatisfied parents

However hard you work to develop good relationships with parents, there will inevitably be some disagreements, misunderstandings and complaints. In a centre with a positive approach to partnership, most incidents will be handled promptly and without bad feeling.

All workers can face an angry parent. It is very important that unpleasant experiences with a few are not allowed to become a negative view of parents in general. Such beliefs are almost certain to show through workers' behaviour (including their body language) and will alienate parents – even those who stop short of losing their temper.

Those centres that cater to families under stress are more likely to face parents who become aggressive under pressure and direct those feelings at workers. Parents may well realise that the source of their anger, perhaps the housing or benefits department, is not the centre's responsibility.

This section is written from the perspective of workers who face angry parents. However, the positive approach described is equally applicable for angry exchanges between staff, or for a manager facing an angry worker.

Individual differences

Some people express anger more swiftly than others. Your experience with a parent may tell you that she winds up quickly, using strong language and large gestures, but calms down just as fast. This familiar pattern may not be unnerving. However, in quieter moments you might need to explain that her anger frightens the children and you want her cooperation that she will talk with you outside the group room in the future.

Other parents may be reticent about expressing dissatisfaction with the centre or worries about their child. Unless you listen carefully, and recognise how this parent approaches any disagreement, you may not realise that she is very annoyed. As well as individual differences, everyone learns patterns that are influenced by cultural traditions. Some communication styles are very direct, with forthright verbal language, strong eye contact and accompanying body language. This approach can be felt as threatening by people whose cultural experience leads them to link this behaviour with loss of control.

Other cultural traditions may stress that disagreement and conflict is to be avoided. Differences of opinion are communicated by words and body language that indicate non-committal and not an outright lack of agreement. The risk here is that a worker of a different cultural tradition may not realise that a parent is seriously concerned or dissatisfied.

Dealing with anger – a positive approach

Workers may have to draw on reserves of patience and energy but should not be expected to take continuous verbal abuse or physical attack. Neither of these unpleasant scenarios should be dismissed as 'just an occupational hazard'. (See also 'personal safety' on page 112.)

Keep calm
Whatever the reason for a parent's anger, workers should not become angry in return. Your reactions to similar situations in your personal life are your

own business. At work you should neither trade insults nor raise your voice more than is necessary to hold the other person's attention.

Listen and understand

Deal with the emotions first. Acknowledge in words that you recognise the other person's anger or frustration; do not belittle their feelings or try to brush away the seriousness. Some parents lose their temper because their courteous first attempts have been ignored and workers have failed to take their concerns seriously. If an entire team shows respect for parents' views and takes responsibility for passing on parent's concerns, then a usually calm parent will not explode from sheer frustration. Other parents may just have a short fuse.

It is not your role to push parents into more serious levels of complaint

Listen carefully to what the parent is saying. Do not rush in with explanations, excuses or direct suggestions. You may reflect back with, 'I can understand that you're cross about Melissa's accident' or 'I appreciate you're worried about Gary's safety, given his disability'.

You are not agreeing that this parent is right (factually) to be angry or worried; you are showing that you recognise their feelings. It would be poor practice to assume that a parent must be wrong. For instance, you might say, 'So, Tina says she was left behind on the common'; you would *not* dismiss the claim with, 'We would never forget a child!'.

Using this approach will be successful in the majority of situations. However, there may be times when you need to speak later, when the parent has calmed down.

Invite information

Use open-ended questions to find out what has happened and how the parent feels. Keep what you say simple and with the aim of hearing the details of what is concerning the parent. There may come a time for explanations or suggestions that the parent has misunderstood an incident, but not yet. When people are angry or upset, they need to know that you care before they are ready to care about what you know. Logical argument especially will not be effective when the other person is expressing strong feelings.

Take appropriate action

When parents have expressed their feelings or calmed down, find out what they would like to have happen; they may have a clear preference. Other parents may want you to know that they are irritated or upset, but have not yet thought about what should be done.

Sometimes an angry parent may be accusing someone else – a child or adult. Do *not* make hasty decisions as to whether a parent is right or wrong. Sometimes you will need to promise to investigate; this commitment should be kept in the very near future. You might reply, 'You say that two children have baited Siobhan about being Irish. I take this matter seriously. Please let me look into it; I will get back to you'.

If there is cause for apology, then make one, but do not apologise just to end the conversation. You might say, 'I'm very sorry. It was inexcusable that our volunteer tried to make Jay eat the meat pie. We know your family is vegetarian'. A suitable follow-up to an apology might be, 'Thank you for telling me. I want to find out how this happened'. Sometimes, it will be appropriate to speak later with a parent with reassurance that the same error will not occur again.

Do not make promises that you may not be able to keep. Sometimes there may not be a workable solution, but parents can see that you are attempting to resolve the issue, even if only in part. Offer information and explanation to the parent if this is a suitable focus. You may need to explain specifically about your aims in work with the children or how centre policy affects what can, and cannot happen.

Refer if necessary

Sometimes workers will be able to deal with disagreements entirely by themselves. However, at other times the most appropriate step will be to refer the parent to someone else. Explain who, within the centre, is the best person to deal with the problem. If at all possible, take the parent to the other person and give a brief summary to ease the transition.

If parents continue to be dissatisfied, explain how they can make a formal complaint (see page 113).

Personal safety

Assertive words and body language are often required. An assertive approach is firm but does not require you to shout. You may need to say strongly to a parent, 'You are frightening the children. Please stop yelling' or 'I will listen to what happened yesterday; I won't listen to insults'.

In any centre, but especially in one with families under stress, there should be a clear agreement between workers on how to support one another if a colleague calls for help or raised voices are heard. Some centres may need to install panic buttons.

In circumstances where there are no other colleagues, for instance in home visiting, workers need to trust their instincts and leave a family home if they judge their personal safety is compromised. Centres that do home visits may choose to send workers in pairs if the district or estate is known to be unsafe.

Reading on . . .

★ Breakwell, Glynis M. 1989: *Facing Physical Violence* (The British Psychological Society/ Routledge).

TO THINK ABOUT

All of the following are legitimate concerns but raise different issues. Note down what you judge would be good practice in handling each of the complaints. Discuss your views with colleagues:

- 'You forgot to give my son his lunch-time medication.'
- 'Why do I have to pay fees when my child isn't here?'
- 'How come her child is here four days a week and you'll only give my son two afternoons.'
- 'I found this bad graze on my daughter's leg. Why didn't you tell me she'd fallen over.'
- 'When are you going to teach them to read? All they do is play around.'
- 'The other kids won't let my son forget that he wet his pants last week. I've got a list of their names and I want them all punished.'
- 'You had a birthday party for my daughter yesterday. We're Jehovah's Witnesses and we don't celebrate birthdays. I explained everything when she started.'
- 'Your Tuesday helper has got it in for my child. She nags her all day long.'
- 'My daughter says that Brian (worker) put his hand up her skirt.'

Keep notes

It is good practice to keep a record of questions raised by parents that challenge how the centre works. Useful information can emerge if a team is willing to look objectively at disagreements that are resolved informally between parents and workers. There may be valuable messages about the expectations raised by the particular wording of the centre's brochure. Or a meeting for parents might address how the centre play programme builds the basis to literacy skills without which children will never learn to read.

Such records must be set up positively in order to avoid any sense of, 'my notes prove that Ujala's father is the worst moaner of all the parents'. Serious incidents, perhaps involving accidental injury to a child while in the centre, would be the subject of a separate investigation and report.

A complaints procedure

A formal complaints procedure needs to be established for every early years centre. However, the majority of everyday questions and criticisms will not be taken on through this route *so long as* minor concerns expressed by parents are handled courteously and promptly by workers. (Workers with a complaint use the grievance procedures – see page 94.)

The complaints procedure should be easily available in written form so that parents can read and understand how the system works (see *'Reading on'* for help in drafting procedures). Any leaflets should be available in the languages spoken by families (see page 2 for some general points about translations). Be ready to explain the process to parents if they are making a complaint and to manage their expectations of what will happen at each step.

The centre will need to have one worker who is responsible for dealing with formal complaints. This person should be a senior worker – in a small centre most likely the manager – or a member of the management committee. The title 'Complaints Officer' sounds rather negative, so the alternative 'Parent Liaison Officer' (PLO) is used in this section.

TO THINK ABOUT

A positively handled exchange with a dissatisfied parent can help to build a good relationship; the result is not always negative. A worker who shows respect for parents' concerns is acting in the spirit of partnership.

Consider recent incidents in which parents expressed dissatisfaction with your centre.

1　Think over an incident that you feel was well handled. Describe how this exchange led to a positive outcome, even if what the parent most wanted was not possible.
2　Think constructively about a less successful incident. What can be learned from the details of communication in this exchange? Some difficulty may have arisen from the parents' behaviour but do not place all the blame on them. How might a similar situation be better handled next time?

The key theme running through this kind of exercise is 'What can we learn?'

A review or appeals panel should handle those formal complaints which the centre is unable to resolve. The panel should remain small, probably no more than three members, and should include one person who has no connection with the centre. Membership should reflect the diversity of families using the service, although in a very diverse area it will impossible to have a representative of all the local ethnic or cultural groups. A panel might be shared with other local centres.

Three steps in complaint

A complaints procedure would usually have three main steps:

1　An attempt to resolve the complaint informally.
2　A system for registering a formal, written complaint.
3　Independent investigation by a panel.

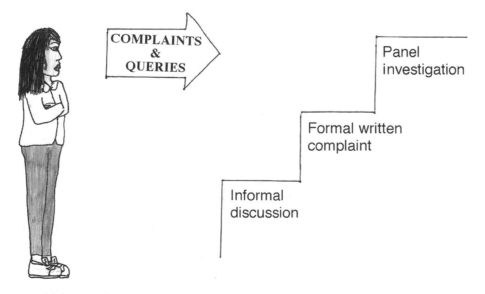

The steps for following a complaint should be clear for parents

1 informal approach

It would be poor practice to have a system which pushed parents into formal complaints when they only wished to talk (see 'A positive approach' on page 110). Part of the informal stage might be to offer parents the opportunity to meet a more senior worker, a member of the management committee or another appropriate professional within the line management of the centre. A senior worker may be able to facilitate a discussion about the problem following the steps to resolving conflict (see page 68).

It would be appropriate, even at this informal stage, to make notes. A copy should be given to the parent if this is a serious complaint. Or, it might be more appropriate, for instance, to show that a mistake has been corrected on a child's file.

Important point: should the complaint reach step 3 and go before the panel, nobody directly involved in handling the complaint earlier can sit on the panel, since its members must be seen to be independent.

TO THINK ABOUT

It can be useful to consider personal experiences of wishing to complain.

1 Think of a few recent incidents when you were dissatisfied with goods or services. Consider one incident in which you feel your complaint, even minor, was well handled and one occasion when you emerged feeling even more dissatisfied or angry with your treatment than before.
2 What happened – what did the other person do and say? Which aspects of the communication were positive and which were negative?

---

2 registering a written complaint

If the informal approach does not resolve the complaint to parents' satisfaction, then they must be given the choice to take their concern to a more formal level. Parents will now have to express their complaint in writing to the Parent Liaison Officer. Some parents may want a friend to help or may need an interpreter.

The written complaint should be registered in the centre's official records. The PLO then investigates the details. There are several important aspects of that investigation:

● If the centre has a management committee, they should be informed (in general terms) that a complaint has entered the formal stage. Full details of who was complaining and the exact nature of the complaint would be kept confidential, because committee members could not hear the case objectively at review stage if they have been involved at step 2.
● If a formal complaint is about the actions of a worker, then that worker must be given the details. Otherwise, keep centre gossip to a minimum.
● Parents should be sent a written acknowledgement of their formal complaint and given details of what will be done and by when.
● The PLO should investigate all details of the complaint, talking in private with everyone involved and making detailed notes. Alternatively the officer can ask someone else to undertake this investigation.
● Within an agreed time span – not usually more than a month – the parent should be fully informed of the results of the investigation and how it is proposed to resolve the complaint.

- If parents are dissatisfied with the proposed solution, then they have a set time, probably a month, in which to decide whether to go to the next stage.

All centre workers are responsible for maintaining a civil relationship with a parent who has complained. Any negative feelings about the parent must not be allowed to rebound on the child. Workers may feel uncomfortable, but should realise that parents may be equally unhappy about the situation. Parents' commitments may leave them little choice but to continue to bring their child to the centre and trust in workers' professional behaviour.

3 review by an independent panel
It is crucial that the panel is seen to be objective and independent: being inclined neither to the centre nor to parents. The panel members will read all the material on the complaint. They will then meet with the parent, and any worker mentioned in the complaint, either of whom can have a friend or advisor to support them.

The panel meeting is serious but should not be allowed to become confrontational. Like any meeting, this review will need the skills of chairing (see page 72). After consideration of all the information the panel reports back to the centre, the parent and worker. The panel's decision may include recommendations. If the decision includes a judgement that a worker's behaviour is unacceptable, steps might then be taken within the centre's disciplinary procedures (see page 94).

Reading on . . .

★   Rogers, Rick 1993: *Sorting Things Out: How to set up and run a complaints procedure* (National Early Years Network).

6 Working well with parents

This chapter covers:

- involvement of parents in the centre;
- running groups for parents;
- working with families;
- home visiting.

6.1 Parent involvement with the centre

Partnership between parents and workers means very little if it exists only as words on a centre brochure. The principle has to be put into practice through daily contact and events within the centre. There are a number of possible ways to offer involvement to parents and no single answer for all centres. Any staff team would have to develop the centre's approach with regard to several key issues:

- What is the overall aim of the centre? A sessional playgroup, a private nursery offering day care and a local authority family centre could not approach parent involvement in exactly the same way.
- What is the range of parents who currently use the service? How can the centre be responsive to their circumstances? For instance, if the parent group includes many with jobs, then patterns of involvement requiring time during the day would place a burden on parents.
- In what ways would parents welcome involvement? What do they see as the key issues?
- How recently has the pattern of parent involvement been reviewed? Patterns should not remain fixed for years. Is what you do still suitable for the centre's aims and the current group of parents?

Inviting parents to stay in the group

Parents can be offered a warm welcome to stay in the group with their child (after settling in) and some will be pleased to accept this invitation. Several practical issues are important if this type of parent involvement is to work as a genuine partnership.

Whose objectives?

Be aware that your reasons for encouraging involvement will not necessarily be the same as parents' reasons for accepting the invitation. You cannot then

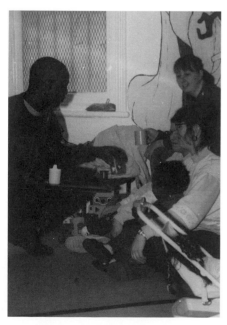

It is a courtesy to offer refreshments to parents as well as children

EXAMPLES – patterns of parent involvement

 1 St Mark's Playgroup

Parents are invited to help in the group. The playgroup used to insist that they joined the rota but this arrangement was discontinued after review in the management committee. Unwilling parents were not beneficial to children's play. Parents interested in helping are asked to make a definite time commitment, so that Sally can plan ahead.

If Sally becomes aware that parents have any special skill or knowledge, she invites them into the group or to share their skill with staff. Parents are asked to all special events and to birthday celebrations for their own child.

The management committee constitution requires that one member is a parent whose child currently attends the playgroup. The committee oversees any fund-raising efforts but particular projects are usually delegated to parents who are happy to take the responsibility.

 2 Salmon Lane Private Nursery

The nursery has a written agreement with parents. It is discussed in the first meeting, then signed by parents and Debbie, the manager.

The nursery caters to working parents, and the approach is to try for friendly contact at the beginning and end of the day, even if the exchange is very brief. Workers are responsible for talking with parents if they have any concern about the child. Depending on the situation, this conversation may be supported by a short letter from Debbie.

Workers attempt to be available for informal conversation when parents wish to talk. If this is a very busy time, then an alternative is suggested. Parents are encouraged to attend a meeting twice a year to discuss their child's progress.

Debbie has started a newsletter that is given to parents every couple of months. The aim is to keep parents up to date with the general themes in work with the children and to give them advance warning of events that they might wish to attend.

 3 Walton Green Family Centre

The centre only takes families through referral from social workers, health visitors or the NSPCC.

The centre's work starts with discussing and drawing up a written agreement of the responsibilities of centre workers and individual parent(s). Some parents agree to spend particular days of the week in the centre, partly with their child but sometimes also as members of a parents' group. The agreement sets specific targets in the joint work and sets a date, not usually more than six weeks ahead, when the agreement will be reviewed.

The staff work as much with parents as with the children. One room is set aside for parents, and a regular group is run by one worker to support parenting skills. Workers are available for informal conversation with parents but the approach of the centre is that longer exchanges are postponed, if only for ten minutes, for an appointment to talk in private.

It is very easy to assume that the pattern of parent involvement of your own centre is the most usual approach.
1 Use the three examples to consider how you put partnership into practice.
2 Visit other local early years settings and discuss their approach.

---

judge the success of having parents in the group against whether the centre's objectives were achieved. Perhaps these objectives were unrealistic: parents' cannot commit the amount of time you hoped. Or you failed to consider the relationship from the parents' perspective: you were hoping to influence how parents relate to their own children but the parents do not see any problem. Clarify both sets of expectations early, through discussion.

Clarity on ground rules and policy

Parents are invited into a centre which already has rules. It would not be honest to suggest parents can follow whatever course of action feels right to them, since this is not true.

Parents would not feel very welcome if they were presented with a long list of 'don'ts'. However, part of making parents feel at ease will be to talk through practicalities such as what they might do in the group, the location of the adult toilets, the time of morning coffee and so on. In the same conversation it is possible to check, for instance, if a parent smokes and to explain the policy on this issue.

Workers will have to step in if a parent is behaving in a way that is contrary to centre policy. For instance, parents cannot deal with children's misbehaviour by hitting them, however strongly they might feel that this action is appropriate.

Respect for parents' approach and skills

Parents may well have a different approach from workers, but the involvement will not be that of a partnership if workers assume that they will always be the ones with expertise.

Parents are a source of skills and ideas. You may find that one parent is an enthusiastic cook and is happy to run occasional cooking sessions for children. Another parent may be an excellent story-teller or know songs and rhymes that are new to you. If you talk with parents, you will discover their areas of knowledge. They may be able to complement the staff team, perhaps providing a broader base for different cultures, language and religion.

If parents and workers do not share a similar social or cultural background, then they may bring very different ideas and priorities to the group. Good practice will be to consider parents' views with an open mind and if possible to integrate these into centre practice.

✠ CASE STUDY

St Mark's Playgroup runs morning and afternoon sessions, but has a group of ten children who stay all day and eat lunch with the playgroup workers.

Himali has joined the full-day group and her mother is spending three days with her to settle her in. At the first lunch time, Himali eats neatly with her fingers, using bread to guide the food. The other children at the table look shocked and four-year-old Sean speaks up: 'That's messy. You're not supposed to eat with your fingers. Sally says that's just for McDonald's'. Himali's mother looks very uncomfortable and reprimands her daughter with, 'Use your knife and fork. Remember what I told you about playgroup'.

The playgroup team discuss the incident at the end of the day. They have difficulty reaching an agreement about how to react to what is Himali's normal way of eating. Philip takes the line that the family lives in England and should eat the English way. Sally and Malaika want to be more flexible, but are concerned at the prospect of a table full of children eating with their fingers – what will their parents say? Anne has said before that the team makes too much fuss about table manners and again brings up her doubts about whether they should be saying grace.

1   What issues are raised by the lunch-time dilemma in St Mark's?
2   What might be the best way forward? With Himali and her mother? In reviewing the playgroup's approach to meals?

Easing parents into the group

Some parents will be quickly at ease in a group. They will have some idea of what they could do and be ready to ask you if they are in any doubt. Other parents may be keen to fit in but are not nearly so confident. Parents often feel more comfortable if you make suggestions about what they could do. For example:

- 'Perhaps you could stay with the sewing group. We like to have an adult with them all the time. The needles are blunt but we still need to ensure safety. And the children often need help when their threads get tangled.'
- 'I'd welcome your help with the painting corner. The children like company and you can get fresh paper and peg up the wet paintings. The paper is on the top of the red cupboard.'
- 'We are about to tidy up now. Could you be with the children who are putting away the bricks? We encourage them to do most of the tidying up themselves.'

Inviting parents to stay in the group is not simply an extra pair of hands for the centre. Be ready to give time and attention to the adults and to deal with any possible conflict in priorities between the needs of parents and children.

Parents who stay may sometimes wish to talk with you as a fellow adult, perhaps about issues with their own child. You need to be tactful in closing down conversations that are dominating your time or which are inappropriate in front of the children. Offer the parent a chance to talk at a better time. If parents find you a sympathetic and helpful listener, they may look to you for guidance. If this involvement takes you towards counselling, you need further training (see the suggested reading on page 83).

Reluctant parents

Not all parents will wish to stay, even if they have no other obligations. It is doubtful whether there will be positive results from pressurising reluctant parents to stay in the centre. Continue to show that they are welcome and share what their child is doing in the group. Offer routes to involvement that do not require a regular presence in the group.

The situation is different in children's and family centres where the focus of the work is on the whole family. If you work in this kind of centre, then the agreements drawn up with parents may require their commitment to spend specific times with their child in the group.

Parent-helpers in the group

Some centres ask that parents help on a regular basis in order to maintain a good adult–child ratio. The manager is likely to want parents to commit to particular days and times so that the play programme and any special events can be planned around a predictable number of adults. Sessional playgroups are most likely to develop this kind of parent involvement. Full-day playgroups are more likely to have working parents who use the group to provide child care. The whole point of the group would be lost for these parents if they had to take time off work to do their stint on the rota.

Successful involvement of parents as regular helpers depends on many of the issues raised in the section on 'inviting parents to stay in the group' (see page 117). A pattern of regular helping can boost the self-esteem of the less confident parents, especially when permanent workers take time to encourage them and draw on their special skills.

It is important that any difficulties are discussed so as not to undermine parents' confidence. Sometimes a parent may not have realised that the group has a particular way of running an activity and as a result is very uncomfortable about the mistake. There may be a lesson for workers about giving more explanation. On other occasions a parent may be taking the approach that is usual in their own home – perhaps that children should remain silent at mealtimes. Explain what is usual in the group and your reasons for choosing that way.

ACTIVITY

A rota of parent-helpers can be a boost for a group. However, any centre has to be sure that health and safety requirements are not being overlooked because of a feeling that parent-helpers are 'not really here officially'.

In your centre, check on the situation over the following:

- Insurance – if, for example, a parent-helper were involved in an accident with a child. Also the insurance situation if the parent were injured.

- Do parent-helpers have the same checks, for instance, health or criminal convictions, as permanent staff? If 'No', how can you justify this?

- What information do you give parents, for example, about a hygienic approach to a child who is bleeding or who has had a toileting accident?

If parents become very involved in the group, then their life may revolve around time spent in and for the centre. Workers should be sensitive to this development, since the end of a child's time in the centre may be more disruptive for the parents than usual (see page 109).

Workers are responsible for behaving in the way that they would wish parent-helpers to follow. Official policy on encouragement of children will be meaningless if a worker has been allowed to slip into habits of nagging or ridiculing the children for mistakes.

Parent-helpers will enjoy a more satisfying time if they are encouraged to work with different groups of children and become confident with a range of play activities. It is not good use of parents' time if they are pushed into all the cleaning and tidying up tasks. Moreover, they will not feel appropriately valued. However, parents should not be covering the full range of tasks that are the responsibility of the permanent staff.

Limits to the work of parent-helpers

Workers need to agree about which tasks should not be delegated to parent-helpers. Good practice includes the following reservations:

- *Records* For reasons of confidentiality, parents should not have access to children's personal records (other than their own child's). Important information about a child's health or well-being should be written in another form that is easily accessible to all the adults. The details should be communicated verbally as well. For instance, parent-helpers will have to know that Pippa must never have any nuts or that Abbas may need his inhaler if he gets very excited.

- *Discussion with other parents* Permanent workers should be the ones to talk with parents whose children have been misbehaving in the group, or if workers are worried about the child for some reason. Any conversations with a parent-helper about a child will have to be conducted with full attention to the family's right to privacy and limits to what should be said to another parent.

- *Visiting professionals* Parent-helpers might have informal contact with a professional who visits the group. A permanent worker should be the main link and should lead in the consideration of how any ideas could be used with the child in the group. The worker should also maintain communication with the child's own parent.

- *Legal or child protection issues* Children and family centres are more likely to be involved in case conferences or legal proceedings. However, it is possible that playgroups – the centres most likely to have regular parent-helpers – may face this situation. A permanent worker should handle matters arising from case conferences or any legal action. Parent-helpers may be involved as witness to an incident.

Parent-helpers should certainly be told if a child is not allowed to be collected by a certain member of the family.

TO THINK ABOUT

Consider the extent to which you have thought through the use of parent-helpers in your setting.

1   Has your team, for instance, considered the points just made? If not, you need to discuss them in your permanent staff group *before* a situation forces a sudden response.
2   All workers should have clear guidelines in their mind about how much is said to parent-helpers about children or families. The decision should not depend on how far you think an individual parent can be trusted.

Other forms of involvement
Supporting the centre

Parents may be active in fund-raising. This type of involvement has a long tradition with Parent–Teacher Associations in schools. Playgroups and after-school clubs may be dependent on fund-raising for extras and special trips. Parents may be involved along with workers or may take the main responsibility for a fund-raising event. Several practical issues arise as a result of the activity being undertaken for the centre:

- The manager, and a management committee, should be kept fully informed of plans. Someone in an official capacity should keep a watching brief.
- Any means of fund-raising must be compatible with the values of the centre and follow any legal requirements, for instance, about running a raffle.
- Workers and parents with prior experience must be honest with 'new' parents about the skills of planning and sheer hard work required for fund-raising events.
- Any fund-raising activity must keep financial records (see section 1.3 for general points about such records).

Activities for parents

Some forms of parent involvement include social activities for children and adults, or just for adults. Some events, such as dances or buffet meals, may also be a means of fund-raising, perhaps largely organised by parents.

Any events that involve food and drink need to be planned with a range of diets in mind. Some parents will not drink alcohol, for personal or religious reasons, so a range of non-alcoholic drinks should always be available. Food should include vegetarian snacks or dishes. It is not very welcoming to vegetarian parents at a summer barbecue to be faced with nothing but hot-dogs and burgers. A practical step is to write clear labels for all dishes. Non-vegetarian parents may avoid some kinds of meat for religious reasons.

A programme of social activities can work well, so long as parents are interested and workers are happy about an extension to their day. The events can be a time for workers and parents to build friendly relationships.

A manager, with any parent organisers, should check on the possible reasons for very low attendance at social events and not just assume that 'parents don't care'. Some parents (or workers) would rather have a social life separate from the centre and pressure to attend will not generate positive feelings. Parents (or workers with children) have to make baby-sitting arrangements, and perhaps pay, in order to get out in the evening. They therefore need early warning of any dates.

The same practical points apply if a centre organises meetings for parents with the aim of sharing information, laying out displays or perhaps with invited speakers. The manager should check that the topic of the meeting is likely to attract parents, ideally by asking them.

Management and decision-making

Good practice in partnership with parents is that all parents are fully informed and consulted on decisions about their own child. Parents may also be involved in decision-making for a centre. For example:

- Individual parents may sit as a parent representative on the management committee or as a parent governor for a school.
- A parents' board, newsletter or suggestions box may offer the opportunity to comment on centre life or to build relationships between parents.
- Open meetings may be held for parents so that they can express their views about the direction that a centre is taking. Such meetings will only work if the chair is honest about the objective of the meeting. Parents are irritated if they attend, believing that their views can influence a decision, and then discover the decision has been taken and the meeting is for information only.

Activities that seek to invite parents' views will not be successful if parents cannot see that comments ever lead to any change. Likewise, the atmosphere

Parents have the ultimate long-term responsibility for their children

will become very frosty if any suggestions or criticisms by parents are met by dismissive or defensive replies.

Reading on . . .

★ Lindon, Jennie 1996: 'Play and early learning' in *The Good Housekeeping Complete Book of Parenting* (Ebury Press). Highlights the different issues that arise for play with children in a family home.

★ Lindon, Jennie 1997: *Working with Young Children* (Hodder and Stoughton).

★ Tizard, Barbara; Mortimore, Jo and Burchell, Bebb 1981: *Involving Parents in Nursery and Infant Schools* (Grant McIntyre). Not a recent book, but the discussion is still highly relevant to early years centres.

6.2 Running groups for parents

Some centres run a regular group for parents to attend. Some of these are only open to parents whose children attend the nursery or playgroup. Centres with a strong community ethos may organise groups that are open to any local parents and to carers such as childminders.

Different types of groups

The aims of parents' groups can be varied and several issues have to be discussed and clarified at an early stage:

- What kind of group seems to be suitable for your centre? What would be your aim(s) in establishing this group?
- What sort of group would parents welcome? A vital step is to talk with parents, if they have not yet expressed any preference spontaneously, and discover whether they would welcome time in a group and what kind.
- Will this group need a worker who will take continuous responsibility for the group? Or would it be more appropriate for a worker to help the group get started and then leave the parents to organise themselves?
- Will it be appropriate that the group, once set up, is closed to new members? Or should it always remain open and welcome new members?

Some of the different types of parents' groups are described as follows.

Coffee and chat

Parents' groups can be very informal and meet at a given time in the week, perhaps in a room set aside for parents. The main aim of the group is social: some company and conversation along with simple refreshments. Some parents welcome this kind of regular activity, especially those whose family and housing circumstances leave them very isolated. The contact may be supportive, perhaps leading to mutual baby-sitting arrangements and friendship outside the centre.

Fund-raising groups
Informal parents' social groups may choose to develop into planning and fund-raising groups to support the life of the centre. This type of group will not work unless parents are motivated and able to deal with the organisation required in fund-raising. Sometimes, such a group is very dependent on a few key parents who are happy to devote a great deal of time to the work. The group may fade away when these parents move on with their children.

Activity focus
Some parents may be keen to join a group which focuses on learning specific skills or knowledge. Depending on the interests of parents, a centre might run a group on cooking, crafts or learning a second language. Such groups need a suitably skilled person to run the group.

Informative meetings
Another group for parents may include the social side but also have the focus that particular topics are discussed at each meeting and local professionals are sometimes invited for information and question sessions. Parents should be fully consulted about possible topics and speakers.

Self-help and support groups
Parents' groups may also meet as an opportunity to talk in confidence about particular issues, for example, child care or family life. This type of group might be organised for parents with specific difficulties or distressing life experiences. The aim would be that the group supports and helps individuals.

In your own centre you may find that only one or two of the different types of group are appropriate. You have to consider parents' expressed interests and their motivation to join a group. It is unwise for workers to spend time planning, without checking that the kind of group envisaged is likely to be acceptable to a large enough number of parents.

Running effective groups

Practical issues
A successful and lively parents' group looks deceptively easy to run, yet there are many practicalities underlying the smooth organisation and workers need specific skills to facilitate groups.

- Any group needs to know in advance where it will meet; ideally this is the same room each time. The room should be at a comfortable temperature and have enough space for parents to spread out. It is preferable that there are enough chairs, although parents may be happy to sit on cushions (ask them).
- You need to ensure access for any parent with disabilities that affect their mobility. For instance, could a parent in a wheelchair get in and out of the room with relative ease?
- A group often runs in a more friendly manner if simple refreshments are available – tea, coffee or fruit juices and biscuits. If there should ever be snacks such as sandwiches, make sure that there is a range of fillings to cater to different diets, for instance some that are suitable for vegetarians.
- Parents in a confidential support group might be personally reminded of a regular meeting time, whereas an open group might be promoted by posters in the centre or a general letter to all the parents.

- Any group should have a start and finish time for both parents and workers to enable them to manage other commitments.

Practical issues are important because getting them right avoids predictable problems and gives a message about valuing the parents' group. Parents will conclude, correctly, that their group is of a low priority if meetings are cancelled at short notice or they are pushed out of their normal meeting room to make way for another activity.

Group facilitation

No group should be started unless you can guarantee the appropriate amount of time and attention from the team. It is preferable that one worker should take responsibility for a group, even one with mainly social aims. A fund-raising parents' group might meet sometimes without a worker but there should be regular communication, probably with a named link worker.

In a centre with a number of parents' groups, two or more workers might be involved on a regular basis. Having the same member(s) of staff present in the group will provide continuity and help to build trust between parents and the worker(s). If it does become necessary for a different worker to take over the responsibility, then the transition should be handled with courtesy and a note to parents.

The worker who is responsible for a parents' group needs to draw on good communication skills and assertiveness in order to run an effective and positive group:

- Any group needs to reach a shared agreement on how the group will run. In social groups this may be an informal discussion about practicalities such as timing and making sure that all the cups are washed up.
- Groups in which parents are discussing personal issues need a clear agreement about confidentiality. It is important that each individual parent commits *out loud* to keeping confidential what is heard within the group. Workers are in a different position and should be honest about the fact that some issues may have to be raised with the parent and perhaps another worker outside the group. Parents who gossip will have to answer to the group, and the worker will have to defuse what may be an angry exchange.
- The worker will be responsible for supporting all the parents in contributing to the life of the group as they wish. Part of the worker's task may be to ensure that a parent with very firm views does not dominate the discussion. (See tips for meetings on page 74.)
- Sometimes a parents' social group becomes an exclusive group that is unwelcoming to any new members. It can also happen that an informal group of parents takes over the parents' room. These sorts of group should be open to new members and you may have to act deliberately to bring in and support other parents in order to break up the exclusive clique.
- There is justification for a support group to be closed, or at least that the addition of new parents is discussed. It can take time for trust to build and the entry of new members may disturb the progress of the group's work.
- A manager would need to consider carefully any request from parents for a closed group that defined its membership according to cultural identity or gender. A request might come, for instance, for a fixed number of meetings for black parents to explore their concerns about raising children with a positive identity when they are bound to meet racism.
- The pattern of any group should be reviewed from time to time. Confidential groups need an agreement to meet a specific number of times and then to review how well the group is working for everyone. Self-help

and support groups in centres may eventually have a long life. But this longevity should be deliberate and not the result of never having addressed the issue of 'How long do we keep meeting?'.

Reading on . . .

For an account of a wide variety of parents' groups read:
★   Whalley, Margy 1994: *Learning to be Strong: Setting up a neighbourhood service for under-fives and their families* (Hodder and Stoughton).

6.3 Working with families

Family dynamics

It is more accurate to see the family as an entire unit and not just as separate individuals – adults and children. All families, not only those who are having difficulties, experience a complex system of relationships within the family and with people outside. Every family develops patterns that determine:

- the different roles that adults and children take on in this family;
- how power and authority is balanced;
- the boundaries and limits within which family members operate.

Time spent with the adults in a family can show how a child's behaviour is shaped by family life. All families go through some difficult times and adjustments. Those who cope well will deal with the more negative feelings without assigning blame entirely to one or two members of the family.

EXAMPLE

If parents or workers are experiencing difficulties with a child then it will be less effective, as well as unjust, to focus only on the child's behaviour. In your centre you may not undertake family work, as such, but an awareness of family dynamics could help you to make better sense of what is happening.

- For some parents, difficulties arise from a baby's or child's natural development. Perhaps Ria's parents were thrilled with a contented and immobile baby but are stunned now that Ria can crawl and is 'wrecking' their immaculate home. They ask for advice now that Ria is 'so naughty', but are very resistant to suggestions to remove the plants and ornaments from their daughter's reach.

- Some families may relish having a child who is a serious handful. The drama of the difficulties may add spice to family life as well as satisfaction that not even the 'experts can do anything with him'.

- A difficulty with one child may 'solve' another problem in the family. Caroline's mother complains that the child insists on sleeping with her each night but she does not use any of the suggestions from the key worker. One consequence of the sleeping arrangements is that Caroline's father sleeps on the sofa most nights. The problem with her child is enabling this mother to avoid facing difficulties relating to her partner.

Supervision and training

It can be hard to remain objective, and workers can sometimes be drawn into family conflict or dealing with the complexities of how one family communicates with its individual members. In any centre where there is work with parents as well as children, the supervision system is especially important to support workers. Additional training in family work is necessary for any staff who are expected to work with the whole family.

Agreements in work with parents

Children and family centres work with both parents and children, rather than providing a service primarily for the children. An agreement is needed between the centre and parents when the individual conditions for the place are established. (See page 98 for agreements in a nursery or playgroup.) The details of the agreement will differ between families but should cover the following general issues:

- What is the centre (and other involved professionals) hoping to achieve with the family through this service? What are the goals?
- For what are the parents asking? What do they hope the service will provide?
- What exactly is being offered – to the child? – to parents? What services, when and for how long?
- How do the parents feel about what is being offered? Do they have reservations? If so, what?
- When will this agreement be reviewed? (A date and time for the review meeting and who will be there.)

The agreement needs to be written up and signed by parent and manager. A copy should be given to the parent(s).

Reading on . . .

Stephen Murgatroyd and Ray Woolfe, have written two useful books:

- ★ 1982: *Coping with Crisis: Understanding and helping people in need* and
- ★ 1985: *Helping Families in Distress: An introduction to family focused helping* (both published by Harper and Row).

Help with the skills of parenting

It is not possible to work on parenting skills simply by bringing parents into an early years centre and hoping they will copy the workers. Parents who are uncertain about their skills may not see how the workers' approach could help them in their own home. Sometimes this reservation is realistic, since early years centres are not family homes.

Parents who experience difficulties

Some parents can be very uneasy about their ability to cope with their children. Their confidence may have been knocked by serious criticism from within their own family or by early years professionals who have suggested, perhaps realistically, that the parents are not caring well for their children. Some parents may already have had children temporarily in care as the result of family difficulties.

Other parents may genuinely have very little idea of what to do with babies and young children or how to safeguard their well-being. For instance:

- Perhaps the parents are still very young – teenagers who find themselves with a baby when they still have not done all their own growing up.
- Some parents may have serious learning disabilities that mean it is difficult for them to understand a child's perspective or to grasp the details of routines for babies and young children.

Adverse circumstances in the lives of some parents may be affecting their ability to focus positively on their children.

- Severe worries about money or housing conditions may dominate an adult's life leaving little energy for the children. Depression, for whatever reason, can incapacitate adults in their ability to run their own lives, let alone allow for the needs of children.

- Past experiences, perhaps traumatic events in parents' own childhood, may be leading them to have serious difficulties as a parent. Perhaps the parents were themselves in residential care for most of their childhood and are trying to make sense of how family life should be run.

Workers will need some understanding of parents' personal circumstances or difficulties in order to adjust their level of support for learning parenting skills. If you work directly with parents it will be important to assess where and how best to put your energy.

If parents are motivated and keen to learn, you may be able to focus directly on their skills with their own child. Yet, a careful assessment of parents' situations may lead you first to offer support in tackling other circumstances. You may not be able to help directly with housing problems or the consequences of a disrupted childhood. However, you could support the parent to make contact with another department or professional who has the relevant expertise.

Reading on . . .

It is important to know your own area well and keep an up-to-date book of local services and contacts. You will find useful general information in:

★ 1995: *Matching Families and Benefits: A handbook for those who support families and young children* (National Early Years Network).

Beliefs about care of children

The right way to raise children

Parents may have strong beliefs that influence the options in their family life. Workers need to understand these beliefs, through conversation, or else their attempts to help parents may be misplaced. Some key beliefs are shaped by parents' religious faith or cultural traditions, but any family will also have an individual pattern. If you talk with parents you may find out why they are loath to follow your suggestions. Further conversation may help you to introduce alternative perspectives. For example:

- Parents may have very fixed views that children 'should' do as they are told, at one asking and with no explanation. 'Good' behaviour from children is defined as following what an adult says without question.
- Families may have different expectations for sons and daughters, so that what is regarded as a problem with a girl is not a source of concern about a boy, and vice versa.
- Some cultural traditions, including those affecting many English families, place more emphasis on punishing wrong-doing than on encouraging children's 'good' behaviour. Suggestions about using incentives may be dismissed as 'bribery'. An approach of ignoring some behaviour may be rejected as 'letting them get away with it'.

Quick solutions?

Some parents, perhaps many, expect that advice from an early years professional will offer an easy solution to a difficulty. Sometimes there may be a simple, practical suggestion. Perhaps an inexperienced mother is holding her baby at an awkward angle for feeding and a slight shift in position makes them both far more comfortable. However, much of daily life with babies and young children is part of a more complex pattern of relationships. For instance:

- Good ideas do not necessarily work first time and parents often need to persevere. Suppose a four-year-old has learned that throwing a tantrum is a sure route to getting her own way, especially in public. She will need more than one experience of her parents' standing firm and refusing to be embarrassed. Her tantrums may even get slightly worse before she realises that the rules have changed.
- A different approach from a parent does not operate like magic to change things forever. Sometimes parents need to change their way on a permanent basis. A bored child who creates havoc at home may be delighted that his parent spends a long playtime with him. He is happily absorbed and so does not empty out the drawers or rip up books. However, the playtime is a pattern that needs to be established for each day; it is not a single-dose solution.
- Good ideas have to allow for family circumstances. There are a number of ways of trying to improve the sleeping patterns of a very wakeful baby or toddler. However, the approach that suggests parents let their child cry for short periods before going in may be impractical for families whose home has thin walls and complaining neighbours.

Parents' knowledge about children

Parents will be supported in their skills of parenting by full involvement and consultation on all aspects of their children's development. All centres should involve parents in this way and parents whose confidence is low can be specifically supported.

Discussions about own child

All centres should keep records of children's developmental progress and this information should be shared with parents. When parents are less knowledgeable about children, then it is especially important to use this information in the most positive way possible:

- Highlight a child's progress over time and explain improvements, even if the child is still delayed or has specific difficulties.
- Explain how workers are helping a child and discuss what parents could do in straightforward and practical language.
- Place any discussion about a child's development or behaviour in the context of level of maturity, including age. Use examples to highlight what are realistic expectations of babies and young children.
- Ask for parents' opinions and invite them to contribute their observations of their child – both at the centre and at home. Focus on what the child does well and avoid an imbalance in the conversation towards problems.
- Involve parents in observation and assessment of their child, perhaps explaining how to stand back and see what a child can do without prompting.
- Encourage parents to attend meetings about their child and make it easy for them to contribute ideas and to join in the discussion of possibilities, as well as making any decisions.

Issues in helping parents to learn

Parents who are having difficulties in parenting will not extend their skills simply as a result of being told what to do by workers, nor will they benefit by being given a copy of suggestions, however good, from another professional, such as a speech therapist or psychologist. An effective approach has much in common with coaching other workers (see page 90).

Recall how much you have learned

You will not have to remind yourself how to communicate affectionately with young children or the value of guiding a young child away from temptation rather than just saying 'Stop it!'. Yet, you were not born knowing all this; you *learned* how to deal positively with children. What may seem very obvious to you now is far from obvious to some parents. You can only help parents in the skills of relating well to children by being very alert to what you do and why you behave this way. Specific examples are usually more helpful than general comments.

One step at a time

You have to decide on the best focus for individual parents in how they could extend their skills. What might be appropriate goals for them? What aspects of their relationship with their child are they concerned to improve? What do the parents already understand? What are they able to do well?

If parents have very low self-esteem, then you may need to be very encouraging to convince them that they could manage their child more positively and that you will support them as they make the effort. Seek to give them an early experience of success.

Motivating parents to change

For anyone to learn, both ability and motivation are crucial. Parents might understand an approach that you discuss and demonstrate, yet be unwilling to follow it. (See 'Beliefs about care of children' on page 131.) Your primary task might be to boost a parent's motivation. For example:

- Some parents may need encouragement to believe that change is possible in a relationship with children. Patterns may not shift immediately but effort will pay off in the end.
- Family life could be more enjoyable with a child who is easier to manage or who delights in the company of a parent who now plays with her far more.
- Sometimes it will be necessary to talk a parent round to acknowledging that there is cause for concern. For instance, a three-year-old who does not talk cannot be dismissed as 'just lazy' or a four-year-old who attacks other children at random should not be indulged as 'a real boy'.
- There can be a particularly serious undertone to the work in children's and family centres and that of family support workers (see also page 137). There will often be serious concern about parents' ability to cope with their child. If specific work with parents does not bring about change, care proceedings may be a possibility.

When talking with parents, seek to stress the disadvantages of the present patterns and alert them to the future benefits of putting time and effort into changing their ways with their child. Parents will often need to see the personal advantages of making a change.

Ways of helping

Whether you are working with parents within the centre or visiting them at home, there are a number of approaches to helping with parenting skills.

Showing

It can be very helpful to demonstrate to parents how you care for or play with children, so long as this approach is also supported by talking with and listening to the parents.

Sometimes it will be appropriate to talk through what you are doing. For instance, an inexperienced parent might be watching you feed her baby and it might feel right to comment, 'Can you see? He's trying to hold the spoon. It won't be long before he's feeding himself'. Or you might alert the mother to the kind of precautions you take as a matter of course by saying, 'Did you see how he managed to roll over? That's why I have everything close to the changing mat. I don't turn away, even for a moment'. Any comments need to be phrased so that parents are drawn into what is happening and invited to take an interest. Showing will not be an effective approach if it is accompanied by a patronising form of telling.

Showing parents will be most effective if there are plenty of opportunities for parents then to try out different ways of relating to their children. Practice is crucial for learning. Sometimes workers deliberately stand well back to allow parent and child time together. A parent with little confidence may wish you to be close, but the time must come when you say, 'You try it now'. Then give honest, supportive feedback.

TO THINK ABOUT

Sometimes, parents may need time to explore play themselves before they can benefit from your showing them how to play with their own child. Parents whose childhood was disturbed or very disrupted may have few happy play memories of their own.

The play materials in your centre may delight parents for whom they are new. Adults may effectively compete with the children for the building or craft materials and then compete for workers' attention. The best way to deal with such a situation will be to create a space, or even a parent's craft group, that allows them to explore skills and find pleasure in what they make.

Talking and listening
You may talk with parents while you are sharing or taking turns in care and play with their child. There will also be opportunities to talk about some incidents or play opportunities after the event. You might have an informal conversation with some parents, whereas others might prefer regular times to talk in confidence. Sometimes discussion can occur within a group run for parents. Any exchanges have to be two-way and not a lecture at parents.

- You might discuss an incident with a child that did not go perfectly, so that parents can understand that you do not have superhuman powers. Perhaps it took you some time to deal with a tantrum or you apologised to a child after you made a mistake. Sharing these experiences may help a parent to understand that nobody is perfect with children; you do your best.
- It may help to talk through the likely consequences of different adult behaviour and explain, for instance, your reasons for thanking children for their help rather than simply assuming they should do it anyway.
- Invite parents' comments and thoughts, including their beliefs about how children should be treated.
- Any of your suggestions need to be given in a straightforward manner in everyday language and not professional terms. In most cases, the choice as to whether to follow any advice will rest with parents, who have to accept the consequences of not facing a difficulty.

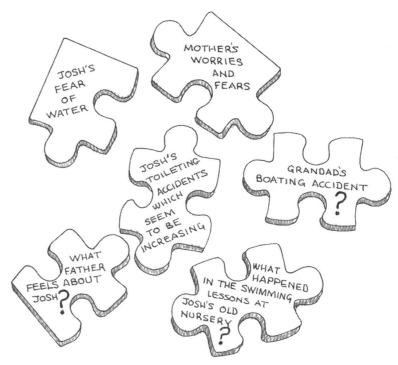

You will not always know the whole story – do your best to help through what you do understand

Parents of children with special needs

When children have disabilities, parents face an additional drain on their skills and energy. In the case of young children there may still be uncertainty about the diagnosis and likely development. Parents may hope that something extraordinary will happen or perhaps one parent is refusing to accept reality. Parents face the task of adjusting family life, perhaps including other children, to the needs of a child with severe disabilities.

Centre workers can be an invaluable support to parents who are trying to weigh up well-meant advice from several different professionals, or even suggestions that are contradictory. You may support some parents who are convinced, correctly, that something is the matter with their child but are having immense difficulty in obtaining appropriate professional help.

You may help parents with some very specific parenting skills appropriate to the needs of their child. Recognise, however, that some parents become out of necessity, an expert in their child's condition and how it affects her.

Reading on . . .

★ Cunningham, Cliff and Davis, Hilton 1985: *Working with Parents: Frameworks for collaboration* (Open University Press).
★ Davis, Hilton 1993: *Counselling Parents of Children with Chronic Illness or Disability* (British Psychological Society).
★ Kerr, Susan 1993: *Your Child with Special Needs* (Hodder and Stoughton).

General support

Sometimes parents may need further information or could benefit from contact with other organisations or self-help groups. Any centre should have a regularly updated file of local groups and useful contacts within services for the early years (see also Appendix 2). You may be able to support parents as they make contact or to ease their entry into a group. Some parents will be able to search out the relevant contact, once you have shared the initial information. A lively parents' group in a centre may form their own network – supporting each other, keeping others company if they wish and sharing information.

Reading on . . .

★ Hartley-Brewer, Elizabeth 1994: *Positive Parenting: Raising children with self-esteem* (Cedar).
★ Smith, Celia 1996: *Developing Parenting Programmes* (National Children's Bureau).
★ Smith, Celia and Pugh, Gillian 1996: *Learning to be a Parent* (Family Policy Studies Centre).

CASE STUDY

Walton Green Family Centre has a number of parents who are attending with their child(ren) for at least some of the days. The following parents have joined the centre within the last six weeks:

- Natalie has three-year-old twins whom she finds very hard to manage. The boys' father is married, with another family, and makes infrequent visits. Natalie's mother helps her out but is very critical of how her daughter deals with the boys. Natalie was willing to attend Walton Green so that 'experts' could discipline the twins. She arrived convinced that it was too late to change anything about her chaotic life with the boys.
- Wayne and Allison are seventeen-year-olds with a ten-month-old baby, Robbie. They keep to their agreement to come every day, although they are sometimes late. They have understood that there is a strong possibility of care proceedings, if they do not learn how to care for Robbie. Wayne and Allison are very affectionate towards their son and do not want to lose him. But they often forget about feeding and changing the baby and are uncertain how to deal with him now that Robbie is more mobile.
- Dawn is twenty-two and has two children with different fathers. She spent most of her childhood in and out of residential care. Dawn has agreed to attend with her youngest child, who is not yet in school. She spends time in the group with her daughter, Anna, and in the parents' group. Dawn says very little unless asked a direct question. She has taken an interest in the craft materials, but wants to create her own work rather than play with Anna.
- Ella has a serious drinking problem. The agreement is that she will attend the alcohol dependence unit on two of the four days that her daughter, Whitney, comes to the centre. Ella wants time from workers to discuss events from her childhood that she says caused her problems. Her accounts vary and it is hard to assess where the truth lies. Ella quickly becomes angry if a worker does not give her immediate attention. Recently she lunged at Andrew, who was reminding her to spend time in the group with Whitney. This week she discovered the home address of Anouska, her key worker, and turned up on Saturday morning insisting that Anouska take Whitney for the weekend.

1 What are the main issues that are raised by each of these examples?
2 What could be the needs of the children and the needs of the parents? To what extent will workers have to address these separately?
3 What could be realistic goals to set in the work with each parent?

6.4 Home visiting

Single home visits

Early years workers may visit parents at home because the home visit is part of the process of introducing parents to the centre once a child has been offered a place. The advantage of this type of home visit is that workers see children in their home surroundings and later contact with the parents may be more effective because workers understand the family circumstances. The meeting can be more personal in someone's home, even when the centre office has been furnished and organised to be very welcoming.

Workers have to be cautious about any conclusions they draw from home visits. Parents who are uncommunicative may be hostile, but it is just as likely that they lack confidence or are concerned about the presence of someone official in their home. They may be worried that you are judging them – a view that has some basis. Homes may be empty of toys because a parent is concerned that you see a tidy home and children may be told to keep quiet because the parent wishes you to think they are well-behaved.

Any centre has to weigh up the possible advantages and disadvantages of meeting parents first through a home visit. An experienced worker may well be able to put a parent and child at ease, but some parents may prefer to visit the centre for this meeting.

Family support workers (FSWs)

The job of family support workers is to visit parents and children in their own home over a period of time in order to help them with some aspect of family life or child care. FSWs have to work with the realistic possibilities of the family home and may be talking with a parent while other relatives are present or competing with a range of domestic distractions.

Families may be referred to an FSW through a social worker or health visitor. Some parents refer themselves, for instance by hearing about the service through a friend.

The personal element

There are common themes for an FSW and staff in centres who work closely with parents (all of this chapter is relevant to family support work). However, a significant difference is that the FSW is going into the family's home territory, so has to accept these circumstances and adjust the work accordingly. It is important to show respect for the choices of different families. Yet concern for the child(ren) may lead to making firm suggestions to parents and including, in written reports, concerns for a child's safety or well-being.

There is an element of befriending in the role of an FSW. However, you are still there in a professional capacity, with a responsibility for reporting to your line management on the progress of the work. Other professionals involved with the family also need to be kept informed. Such a relationship needs to be faced honestly with the family. An FSW can face conflict between respecting the confidences of a parent and professional obligations.

A family support worker may relate to several members of a family

An individual approach

The focus of work will vary for each family and should be part of an agreement that is made with the parents in the early stage of the working relationship.

As with any kind of close work with families, you may find that some parents, or other relatives in the home, are resistant or openly hostile to your presence. It will sometimes be necessary to be satisfied with working well with one member of the family if the results are positive for the child(ren).

FSWs may be told personal information as the relationship grows but details should only be explored in order to help parents resolve difficulties or learn new skills with their children. Individual parents will have to work at their own pace and on tasks that they are motivated to face. There will be little point in FSWs trying to push parents beyond their own limits. Part of the task for a support worker may be to judge the limits of a parent's capability when quality of care of a child is in doubt.

Professional support

Home visiting can be an isolating job and it is crucial that your department or organisation allows time for you to discuss and consult on your work with families. There should be regular opportunities to meet with other support workers in your organisation and to have supervision from your line manager or someone else appropriate for the task. It must be very clear to whom you report any serious worries about a child. This system must be well established regardless of whether the FSW is paid or is working on a voluntary basis. Home-start UK, for instance, has supported local schemes in which volunteers, usually parents, are trained before they start home visits to families with difficulties.

Families should be told to what extent their family details will be passed to any other professionals. In the same way as a centre worker, FSWs have to make careful judgements to ensure that information is not passed onto other professionals or organisations without good reason and the parents' permission.

Most home visits will be made by a single FSW. Personal security, as well as good record keeping, requires keeping a log of your planned visits, with addresses and times. Since families are expected to keep to their side of agreements, it is important that FSWs are punctual and keep appointments. Any changes should not be at short notice unless there is a very good reason.

Reading on . . .

For some of the different kinds of home visiting schemes read:
★ Pugh, Gillian; De'Ath, Erica and Smith, Celia 1994: *Confident Parents, Confident Children: Policy and practice in parent education and support* (National Children's Bureau).

For a description of home visits as part of the work of a centre, see:
★ Whalley, Margy 1994: *Learning to be Strong: Setting up a neighbourhood service for under-fives and their families* (Hodder and Stoughton).

Appendix 1: NVQs/SVQs

The full details of the NVQs/SVQs are given in *National Occupational Standards for Working with Young Children and their Families.* If you are studying for your NVQ/SVQ qualification, you should be able to consult this publication at your college or assessment centre. The complete standards can be purchased from the Local Government Management Board, Arndale House, The Arndale Centre, Luton, Bedfordshire LU1 2TS, *tel.* 01582 451166.

This workbook especially supports the following endorsements at Level 3:

A. Group care and education
B. Family day care
C. Pre-school provision
D. Family support.

The content of the book also supports two Level 2 endorsements:

C. Work in a pre-school group
D. Work in a community-run pre-school group.

The individual units are listed below so that you can turn to the most relevant sections in the book.

Level 3 core units	Sections of this book
C15 Contribute to the protection of children from abuse	1.1, 1.2, 2.4, 5.2, 6.3, 6.4
M2 Carry out the administration of the provision for a care/education setting	Ch. 1
M4 Work with colleagues in a team	1.1, Ch. 3
M6 Work with other professionals	1.1, 2.4, Ch. 3
M7 Plan, implement and evaluate activities and experiences to promote children's learning and development	1.2, 1.5
M8 Plan, implement and evaluate routines for young children	1.2, 1.5, 2.4, 3.3
M20 Work with/to a management committee	1.1, 2.4, 4.1, 4.4
P2 Establish and maintain relationships with parents of young children	1.4, Chs 5, 6
P3 Involve parents in play and learning activities with young children	5.1, 5.2, 6.1
P4 Support parents in developing their parenting skills	5.1, 5.2, 6.3
P5 Involve parents in a group for young children	1.4, 5.2, 6.1
P7 Visit and support a family with young children in their home	2.4, 5.2, 6.3, 6.4
P8 Establish and maintain arrangements with parents for the provision of child care service	1.4, Ch. 5
P9 Work with parents in a group for young children	5.1, 5.2, 6.1

Appendix 2:
How to find out more
– useful organisations

Action for Sick Children
Argyle House
29–31 Euston Road
London NW1 2SD

tel. 0171–833 2041

*Children in Scotland (Clann An
    Alba)*
Princes House
5 Shandwick Place
Edinburgh EH2 4RG

tel. 0131 228 8484

*Children in Wales (Plant yng
    Nghymru)*
7 Cleeve House
Lambourne Crescent
Cardiff CF4 5GJ

tel. 01222 761177

Children's Legal Centre
University of Essex
Wivenhoe Park
Colchester
Essex CO4 3SQ

tel. 01206 873820 (advice line)

Children's Play Council
8 Wakley Street
London EC1V 7QE

tel. 0171–843 6016

Council for Disabled Children
8 Wakley Street
London EC1V 7QE

tel. 0171–843 6061

Early Childhood Unit
National Children's Bureau
8 Wakley Street
London EC1V 7QE

tel. 0171–843 6079

Family Centre Network
NCVCCO (National Council of
    Voluntary Child Care
    Organisations)
Unit 4
80–82 White Lion Street
London N1 9PF

tel. 0171–833 3319

Kids' Clubs Network
Bellerive House
3 Muirfield Crescent
London E14 9SZ

tel. 0171–512 2122

London Voluntary Service Council
356 Holloway Road
London N7 6PA

tel. 0171–700 8107

National Early Years Network
77 Holloway Road
London N7 8JZ

tel. 0171–607 9573

*National Private Day Nurseries
    Association*
Dennis House
Hawley Road
Hinckley
Leicestershire LE1 0PR

tel. 01455 635556

National Society for the Prevention of Cruelty to Children
NSPCC National Centre
42 Curtain Road
London EC2A 3NH

tel. 0171–825 2500

Pre-school Learning Alliance
61–63 Kings Cross Road
London WC1X 9LL

tel. 0171–833 0991

For PLA publications contact *PPA Promotion*
45–49 Union Road
Croydon CR0 2XU

tel. 0181 684 9542.

Video Arts Ltd (produces videos and booklets on many aspects of management)
Dumbarton House
68 Oxford Street
London W1N 9LA

tel. 0171–637 7288

Working for Child Care
77 Holloway Road
London N7 8JZ

tel. 0171–700 0281

Working Group Against Racism in Children's Resources
Lady Margaret Hall Settlement
460 Wandsworth Road
London SW8 3LX

tel. 0171–627 4594

For more information on useful organisations you can consult:
Organisations Concerned with Young Children and their Families: a National Directory 1995, published jointly by National Children's Bureau and National Early Years Network.

Appendix 3: How to find out more – books

Allcock, Debra 1993: *Do Yourself a Favour: How to be successful at work* (The Industrial Society).

Andreski, Ruth and Nicholls, Sarah 1996: *Managing Your Nursery – A practical guide for nursery professionals* (Nursery World publication).

Ansari, Khizar Humayun and Jackson, June 1995: *Managing Cultural Diversity at Work* (Kogan Page).

Cowley, Liz 1991: *Young Children in Group Day Care – Guidelines for good practice* (National Children's Bureau).

Dobson, Ann 1995: *How to Communicate at Work: Making a success of your working relationships* (Kogan Page).

Finch, Sue 1993: *Setting up a Day Nursery: A step-by-step guide* (National Early Years Network).

Garrett, Helen and Taylor, Judith 1993: *How to Design and Deliver Equal Opportunities Training* (Kogan Page).

Johnson, Ron 1995: *Perfect Teamwork* (Arrow).

Kids' Clubs Network 1993: *Guidelines of Good Practice for Out of School Care Schemes* (Kids' Clubs Network).

Petrie, Pat 1994: *Play and Care, Out of School* (HMSO).

Pre-school Learning Alliance 1991: *Equal Chances: Eliminating discrimination and ensuring quality in playgroups* (Pre-school Learning Alliance).

Pugh, Gillian (ed) 1996: *Contemporary Issues in the Early Years: Working collaboratively for children* (Paul Chapman/National Children's Bureau).

Rodd, Jillian 1994: *Leadership in Early Childhood: The pathway to professionalism* (Open University Press).

Rowntree, Derek 1988: *The Manager's Book of Checklists: A practical guide to improve your managerial skills* (Corgi).

Sadek, Elizabeth and Sadek, Jackie 1996: *Good Practice in Nursery Management* (Stanley Thornes).

Steinberg, Derek 1989: *Interprofessional Consultation – Innovation and imagination in working relationships* (Blackwell).

Index